Dear ||||~ ~
you your PROFFEDIONAL
Life. .

From you little, Big Sister!

Gestalt
Counselling

Charlotte Sills
Sue Fish
Phil Lapworth

HELPING PEOPLE CHANGE:
THE ESSENTIAL
COUNSELLING SERIES

Gestalt Counselling

Charlotte Sills
Sue Fish
Phil Lapworth

Speechmark Publishing Ltd

Published by
Speechmark Publishing Limited, 8 Oxford Court, St James Road, Brackley,
NN13 7XY, United Kingdom
www.speechmark.net

002 1945/Printed in Great Britain/1010

British Library Cataloguing in Publication Data
Sills, Charlotte
    Gestalt Counselling. – (Helping People Change: The Essential
    Counselling Series)
    I. Title   II. Series
    616.89143

  ISBN 978 0 86388 369 9
(Previously published by Winslow Press Ltd under ISBN 0 86388 133 5)

CONTENTS

Part IV EXPANSION AND INTEGRATION

PREFACE TO THE SERIES

Welcome to *Helping People Change: the Essential Counselling Series*. Counselling skills are now becoming more and more recognized as an essential part of effective helping. Nowhere is this more true than in social services, education, the health care professions and their associates. In publishing this series Winslow has produced a range of books on different approaches to counselling that should be of immediate practical benefit to anyone in the 'people business'. Each book in the series is written by experienced counsellors respected in their own field. Each title reveals a different way in which you can develop your counselling skills with your clients. I hope you will find them a welcome and close companion in your work.

ROY BAILEY
Series Editor

Charlotte Sills MA, Cert Ed, Advanced Dip Integrative Psychotherapy is a UKCP registered psychotherapist and counsellor in private practice and a trainer and consultant using Gestalt in a variety of mental health settings. She is a certified teaching and supervising transactional analyst and head of the TA Training Department at **Metanoia**, as well as a guest trainer on the Gestalt Diploma Course.

Sue Fish B Soc Sc, Dip Ed, Dip Speech & Drama, Dip NLP & Counselling, Advanced Dip Integrative Psychotherapy is a UKCP registered psychotherapist, a Teaching and Supervising Member of the Gestalt Psychotherapy Institute of Great Britain and a certified teaching and supervising transactional analyst. She has extensive training and experience in remedial therapeutic work with children and young people, including several years as the head of a unit for disturbed adolescents. She was a founder of **Metanoia**, where she practises psychotherapy with children, families and adults, as well as training and supervising in Gestalt.

Phil Lapworth Cert Ed, Dip Counselling Skills, Advanced Dip Integrative Psychotherapy is a UKCP registered psychotherapist, a BAC accredited counsellor and a clinical transactional analyst. He came to counselling through his work in special education in London (as deputy head teacher in a school for children with learning difficulties and as senior teacher at the Maudsley Psychiatric Hospital). For many years director of clinical services at **Metanoia**, he now runs a psychotherapy and supervisory practice in Bath.

All three have been the authors of a number of publications in the field of counselling and psychotherapy. Together they have written *Transactional Analysis Counselling* (Lapworth, Sills & Fish, 1993) – a previous book in the Essential Counselling Series – and *Understand and Use Your Dreams* (Fish & Lapworth, Dormouse Press, Bath, 1994). Their next shared project is *Integrative Counselling*, again in the Essential Counselling Series by Speechmark Publishing Ltd.

ACKNOWLEDGEMENTS

We would like to thank the series editor Roy Bailey for his support and patience during the writing of this book and Tony Waterman for his excellent copy editing. We would also like to extend our appreciation to the friends and colleagues who have been enormously helpful to us: Phil Joyce, whose expert opinion has been invaluable throughout; Jenny Mackewn for her useful and generous suggestions; Ian Greenway for his valuable feedback; Laurie Lapworth for his diagrams; and Janice Scott — counsellor, therapist and trainer at **Metanoia** — for the illustration of Gestalt counselling in practice found in Chapter 14.

A huge thank you to Cathy Chase who was asked to read this book from the viewpoint of an 'ordinary reader', and turned out to be an extraordinary one. We also wish to acknowledge our debt to Dr Petruska Clarkson, whose teaching has been a profound influence in our work. As ever, our most important teachers have been our clients, trainees and supervisees, who continue to enhance our professional lives.

And finally, we thank each other for the fun, warmth and stimulation we have had as we worked together. Sue and Phil would like to give special thanks to Charlotte for her role as main author, which she carried out with generosity and infectious humour.

ABOUT THE BOOK

This book has been written in four parts. Part I is a brief history of Gestalt and its development, followed by an overview of the theory. Part II covers the major principles of Gestalt counselling. Each concept and its application are described, and some exercises are offered for the reader to experience the ideas in action. Part III introduces Gestalt practice, each chapter giving examples of its use and inviting the reader to experiment. Part IV offers a case study example which integrates the theory and practice. It also includes recommendations for enhancing a counsellor's growth, with suggestions for training and further reading.

Part I

BACKGROUND

Chapter 1

A Brief History
of Gestalt

If you are completely new to Gestalt, we suggest that you turn first of all to Part II. This will give you a better idea of the immediacy of the Gestalt approach. Later, you could return to Part I in order to see where it all came from.

The Gestalt approach to counselling was first developed by Frederick Perls (known as Fritz) with his wife, Laura, and other colleagues, in particular Paul Goodman. They brought together a number of different psychological concepts and approaches to develop a method of working with people that was a major challenge to the traditional models of the time, and one that was in tune with the anarchic and free-thinking, anti-establishment mood of the 1960s. Since its growth in America, there have been many developments and refinements of its central theories. Indeed, it continues to develop still, as Gestalt theorists and practitioners continue the tradition of questioning fixed models, and looking at what *is* rather than what is thought to be.

A concept which is central to the Gestalt approach is *wholeness*. In fact the word 'Gestalt' roughly translates from German as 'an organized whole'. It emphasizes looking at whole and integrated experiences — be they groups, objects or individuals — rather than dissecting them into their analysable parts. For example, one could analyse a root, stem, leaf, petal, stamen and pistil, but this would not capture the totality of the flower growing in the ground in a garden. The essential message is that *the whole is more than the sum of its parts*. We will be talking a lot more about wholeness later in this book. For the moment you, the reader, are faced with the first major Gestalt of the book — that of the approach itself. It is made up of many and diverse parts which together constitute the unique whole of Gestalt.

The story of Gestalt therapy starts with Fritz Perls in Germany at the beginning of the century. He was born in Berlin and lived in Germany until 1933. His early life experiences — being a Jew in a non-Jewish area, his anti-Fascist views, his rebellious personality as well as his many areas of study — were all later to affect the approach he developed. After qualifying in medicine, he started training as a Freudian psychoanalyst which he completed in Vienna in 1928. During this time, and afterwards, he underwent several analyses himself. His *psychoanalytic training* had enormous influences on his later ideas. Many psychoanalytic concepts form the foundation of the Gestalt approach. These include the belief that our childhood experiences affect our adult lives; that 'pathological' behaviour has a meaning that may be unconscious but that can be brought into awareness; that humans have natural drives; and that people have an innate tendency towards homeostasis or equilibrium.

Perls was especially influenced by those theorists, sometimes known as 'interpersonal psychoanalysts', who were developing and expanding Freud's ideas towards a more person-centred and holistic approach to clients. These theorists included Fromm, Adler and Rank, and more *radical analysts* such as Reich, who was developing his theory that human problems are manifested not just psychologically but also physically, in 'body armour', and whose work focused on the body and the importance of cathartic expression.

At the same time, Perls was also interested in other movements in Germany, including *Gestalt psychology*, from which the name Gestalt Counselling/Psychotherapy derives. He met and married a Gestalt psychologist, Laura Posner, who taught him much and who contributed greatly to his subsequent work. It was from Gestalt psychology that Perls drew many of his ideas on perception: our perception is geared to seeing wholes, and making sense of the world in whole images or experiences; what is more, of all the potential stimuli we could notice at any moment, we will tend to focus on those which make up a 'whole' relevant to us at that moment according to our perceived needs. For example, the hungry man, faced with a wide variety of items in the kitchen, will notice the bread, cheese and butter, because they will immediately suggest 'sandwich' to him. Only later will he see the note his wife has left him saying his supper is in the fridge. This focus on immediate need has enormous implications for us in our lives, and certainly in counselling.

Another major idea from Gestalt psychology was the 'Zeigarnick effect'. Zeigarnick, a psychologist, first drew attention to the phenomenon that is commonly known as 'unfinished business'. This means that, if we have only some of the elements of a situation or gestalt, we will have a natural urge to provide the rest in order to have completeness. For example, if we write 'elephan' here, you will probably add a 't' automatically in your mind. We are unsatisfied with incompleteness, and things that are not finished for us. Whether they are events, conversations, feelings or our sense of ourselves, they seem to haunt us and have the potential to stop us focusing wholeheartedly on what is happening in the present.

Perls studied *existential philosophy*, which was also to influence his work. Space precludes us from going into the philosophy of those ideas in depth here. It is important to mention, however, that Perls was very affected by the existential notion that human beings, though connected to each other and to every living being, are fundamentally totally separate and alone. This sense of individual aloneness is a sort of freedom that we do not usually acknowledge, imagining ourselves bound to other people in a variety of ways. Being aware of that freedom in a world where we desperately seek meaning can lead to anxiety and despair. But it can also lead to another sort of freedom — the freedom of living authentically without false constraints and obligations, taking responsibility for one's own personal meaning. Earlier, we were stressing the importance of wholeness; here we are emphasizing the separateness of existentialism. It is interesting that both wholeness and separateness are central to Gestalt.

Perls was also involved with *phenomenology*, the study of perception — things as they appear to be. Phenomenology offers a method of becoming aware of and understanding the meanings we are making. It stresses that the only truth we can know is that which is happening in the present moment. This leads to the importance of the 'here and now', which we will expand upon later.

In 1933, the Perls left Germany and after spending a year in Holland moved to South Africa. There, they became interested in the ideas of *holism* put forward by Jan Smuts, the then prime minister. Holism underlines the interconnectedness of all things, as does Lewin's field-theory, and these have become fundamental in Gestalt counselling. *Field-theory* is the bedrock of the approach. It stresses that everything has a context and nothing can be understood separate from its context. Holism also focuses on the natural drive of humans to make wholes and therefore connects well with Perls' views on working in a Gestalt way.

In South Africa also, Fritz and Laura wrote *Ego, Hunger and Aggression* (Perls, 1947). Based on Freudian ideas combined with theories drawn from his other areas of study, the book was the first to put forward Perls' innovative ideas about therapy. It takes the activity of eating (biting, chewing, spitting out, swallowing, digesting) as a metaphor for a person's relationship to the world. He describes aggression as a healthy drive to reach out and take from the world.

Fritz and Laura Perls stayed in South Africa until 1946 when, mainly owing to dissatisfaction with the political situation, they moved to New York. Fritz Perls was then 53. In America they met and worked with many people who were to be important in the growth of Gestalt therapy, amongst them the philosopher and writer, Paul Goodman, and Paul Weiss, who introduced Perls to *Eastern spiritual traditions* and philosophies. Perls was particularly attracted to Zen Buddhism with its emphasis on awareness as being the path to enlightenment. The importance of awareness in the present moment complemented the ideas gleaned from existentialism and phenomenology.

Finally, in exploring the roots of Gestalt it is important to mention the theatre, which had always been a love of Perls. With his penchant for the dramatic, he was very drawn to the work of Moreno, the originator of *psychodrama*, although the two men did not get on personally. In Part III of this book, you will see how Gestalt ways of working can sometimes use the dramatic to heighten the potency of the experience.

Between 1946 and his death in 1970, Perls and his colleagues were involved in the founding and establishing of Gestalt therapy, with important centres in New York, Cleveland, Esalen in California and Cowichan in Canada. His lifetime of travelling made him unwilling to settle in one place, so every few years he moved on to found another centre, leaving his followers to continue the work.

At this point, as Mackewn writes (1994), 'two distinct branches grew out of this integrative and dynamic beginning'. One of these was led by Fritz Perls. He became famous for what he called his 'circuses', where he demonstrated his unique and charismatic form of therapy to full lecture theatres, inviting participants to come and sit centre-stage in 'the hot seat' to work with him. Perls was widely admired and revered for his innovative and iconoclastic ideas and methods. However, while he was described by some people as tender, generous and sensitive, he was much criticized by others for his high-handedness, his arrogance and the abrasive and confrontational manner which could often seem persecutory to his trainees. All in all, the man — like the therapy he founded — was an intriguing, multifaceted whole. If you wish to read more about Perls and the work he did, see Clarkson and Mackewn, 1993 and Mackewn, 1994.

The second branch of Gestalt counselling and therapy was practised and taught by some of Perls' colleagues and trainees and retained more of the rich diversity of sources. Mackewn (1994) lists Gestaltists such as Laura Perls, Fromm, Simkin, Erving and Miriam Polster and Kepner as being significant in the growth of Gestalt in the 1960s and 1970s. Since then, they and others have gone on to develop it further, in terms both of theory and of practice. The year 1977 saw the founding of the American *The Gestalt Journal*, a forum for Gestaltists to debate and develop their ideas.

In these few short pages it has been impossible to convey the depth and complexity of the ideas which grew into the Gestalt approach or the profound effect that it has had on the practice of counselling and psychotherapy. In the past two decades Gestalt has taken a significant place amongst therapeutic approaches in Europe, and European writers are making important contributions to the development of the Gestalt approach. The excellent *British Gestalt Journal* was started in 1991. It is a vital and continuing source of many of the recent international trends and growing edges. It is from the work of many of these recent Gestaltists (to which reference will be made in the text) as well as of Perls and his early collaborators that we have drawn the ideas found in this book.

Chapter 2

AN OVERVIEW OF GESTALT
AND RECENT DEVELOPMENTS

Principles

As we have seen, the practice of Gestalt has grown from a synthesis of many approaches and philosophies. To summarize, these include traditional psychoanalysis, Gestalt psychology, phenomenology, existentialism, interpersonal psychoanalysis, Reichian bodywork, holism, field-theory, Zen Buddhism, psychodrama and the theatre. As we have said, Gestalt theory itself is an example of a Gestalt. Each element stands on its own, yet is part of the integrated theory and practice of Gestalt. The Gestalt understanding of human beings is based upon a number of principles.

Self-awareness

People have the potential to be aware of their emotions, thoughts, sensations and perceptions. In order to make changes in ourselves and our lives (and that is what our clients want to do when they come to see us), we need to develop a freedom to choose new ways of feeling, thinking and doing. Such change can only be brought about by our awareness of our current (and perhaps habitual) ways of being. This awareness in itself can bring about spontaneous change. For instance, a client directing his awareness to a tension in his body can sometimes produce a sudden realization of a previously repressed feeling which can then be expressed.

Wholeness

A person is a whole: body, emotions, thoughts, sensations and perceptions. They all function interrelatedly to create this whole. A graphic example of this is that of the hospital patient who may be 'the kidney case in bed three' but is actually Mary Jones — young, scared, brown-eyed, witty, mother of two — and much more besides.

Self-responsibility

People are proactive rather than reactive. They determine their own responses to the world. Self-awareness offers choices. As we become aware that it is we ourselves who are feeling, thinking and behaving, we take responsibility for choosing how we are, rather than believing "That's just the way I am. I can't do anything about it."

Satisfaction of Needs

People have innate needs and a natural capacity and drive to meet them. These needs may be physical or they may be social. For instance, the need for companionship seems to be universal and most people manage to find enough friends to satisfy that need.

Human Value

People are intrinsically neither good nor bad. We are what we are at any moment. The implication for the Gestalt counsellor is that we move away from judgement towards confirming the client's self-discovery and self-realization.

The Here and Now

'Here' means at the present place and 'now' means at the present time. Sometimes it is said of people that they 'live in the past' or they 'dream away their lives'. How we spend our time is important. People can experience the past through remembering in the here and now, and imagine the future through anticipating in the here and now. We can only be in the present. H.L. Mencken, in *The Little Zen Companion* (1994) said, 'We are here and it is now. Further than that, all human knowledge is moonshine.'

Interconnectedness

People are part of their environment and cannot be understood separate from that environment. Experience always involves our contact with and relationship to our surroundings. Authentic relationships with others are the vehicle for self-actualization. This does not mean that we should define ourselves in relation to others but that we *find ourselves* through that relationship. Clearly, the counselling relationship can provide just such an opportunity.

Figure and Ground

Out of our contact with the environment we vary our focus of perception. Some things will stand out while others remain in the background. In our earlier example, we described a hungry man. As he stood in the kitchen, the ground of his visual experience was the whole of the kitchen. Of all the things in the kitchen, it was the items which meant 'sandwich' that became figure.

Completion

People have a natural tendency to complete experiences, be they events, feelings, thoughts or actions. An unfinished experience or Gestalt will preoccupy us and prevent us from living fully in the present. If you have ever had the experience of wishing that you had said something to someone who has died, you will know how the 'unfinished business' can haunt you.

Self-regulation

Self-regulation is the natural tendency of humans to maintain a state of equilibrium. This includes sweating when we are hot to keep our temperature steady, breathing faster when we are hurrying to provide enough oxygen so that the muscles can continue to function, drinking when we are thirsty, and so on. Hunter Beaumont (1993) prefers the term 'self-organization' as it extends the idea of an organismic tendency to include the functions of thinking, meaning making and organizing ourselves and our world. Thus self-regulation/organization would include 'letting off steam' when we are angry, smiling when we are happy, withdrawing when we feel overstimulated and seeking stimulation when we are bored.

Part II of this book will expand upon these principles as they apply to Gestalt counselling theory, while Part III will focus upon what actually happens between counsellors and their clients.

Recent Trends in Gestalt Counselling

In the 1960s, Perlsian Gestalt counselling and therapy had a dramatic, confrontational feel to it. Clients took the 'hot-seat', not so much to be invited to increase awareness of themselves, but to be precipitated into it, with powerful interventions and techniques. The cultural revolution of that era urged people to throw off their old restrictions and allegiances in order to 'do their own thing', regardless of what others thought. Perls' oft-quoted 'lose your mind and come to your senses' was originally meant to encourage people to stop analysing and thinking about themselves and to start *being* themselves, but it was sometimes taken to extremes as people acted on their impulses without considering consequences. The belief was that clients could be helped to discover themselves and achieve their potential and some of the Perlsian philosophy seemed to suggest that people could achieve this *as individuals*, ignoring the fact that individuals are necessarily involved in relationships and with the wider field of their society.

However, since the early days, and stemming more from the 'second branch' of Gestalt (Mackewn, 1994) there has been a change in emphasis in Gestalt counselling. Amongst others, Rogers, Buber, the Object Relations School and the Self psychologists have had a profound influence on the practice of Gestalt. There has been an increasing understanding of the importance and significance of the relationship between counsellor and client, and a developing belief amongst counsellors that true growth and healing can only take place *in* a relationship, and also that an individual cannot be seen apart from his situation.

In addition, Gestaltists recognized that the more dramatic techniques, while they could sometimes have immediate and powerful effects, did not always produce long-lasting beneficial changes in clients. On the contrary, sometimes the assault on the person's way of being could be experienced as unsettling and undermining. Significant, long-lasting change seemed to be more associated with the respectful and attentive contact between counsellor and client, where — perhaps for the first time — a client may have the experience of being in a relationship where they are truly seen and heard, and where their completeness of self is prized and encouraged.

Gestalt today is an exciting mix, as it always was. At its heart is the therapeutic relationship and a method of exploring and increasing awareness in the dialogue. *Within the context* of this therapeutic relationship, the Gestaltist may invite the client to expand their limitations in a variety of ways that are uniquely Gestalt. It is some of this exciting mix that we hope to convey in the following pages.

Part II
GESTALT COUNSELLING THEORY

Chapter 3

THE COUNSELLING RELATIONSHIP IN GESTALT

We believe that the health and growth of human beings are best facilitated in the context of a relationship. Probably the most important thing a counsellor can offer to clients is a willingness to see, hear and accept them as they are, without preconception, expectation or judgement. By paying respectful attention to our clients' thoughts, feelings and behaviour, we invite them to do the same thing for themselves. We encourage them to become aware of themselves and express themselves as fully as they are able at that time. We act as a witness and in so doing provide confirmation of who they are. As Joseph Zinker (1975) said: 'Our deepest, most profound stirrings of self-appreciation, self-love and self-knowledge surface in the presence of the person whom we experience as totally accepting.' If you have had the experience of feeling wholly seen and heard by someone who has not judged but simply acknowledged what was true for you, you will have felt this profound effect.

Sometimes as counsellors we may think we need to offer our clients sophisticated techniques or theoretical insights which will help them understand themselves. It is important to remember that the counselling relationship may be the first time that our clients have experienced being truly attended to and heard. This experience of confirmation can be the most healing feature of the counselling. Unnecessary interventions or techniques may at times interrupt the healing process. Mackewn (1994) says, 'the power to heal lies not in the therapist or even in the client alone but in what happens between them'.

Why is the relationship so important? Gestalt counselling is not about changing people or telling them what they ought to do. It is not even about encouraging them to change themselves. Gestalt believes that human beings — even those in distress over difficulties — are best able to grow and take charge of their lives by becoming more aware of who they *are* in all their needs and wants, feelings and thoughts, their ambivalences and conflicts, what they say and what they do. Only then can they feel responsible for their own lives and make choices in order for them to find the best resolutions to their problems.

If a person is to have a better awareness of who they are, they must have a clear sense of 'I' — what is 'me' and what is 'not me'. Have you ever been in a flotation tank? You are immersed in warm (body temperature) water in the dark and the quiet, and very soon you begin to feel as if you were at one with the universe. The warm water supports and surrounds your body until it is hard to tell where your body ends and the water begins. This may be an experience close to that of a baby inside a womb. You have some sensation inside you, but no sense of the size, shape or position of your body and limbs — no clear sense of yourself. In order for us to feel ourselves as solidly separate, we need to have something that is obviously 'not us' impinging upon us, touching our boundary, such as the touch of something on our skin or other impressions on our eyes, ears and so on.

Psychologically, a clear sense of ourselves happens in the same way. A person can only define himself as 'I' and have a solid sense of who that is, when that 'I' is in relation to something which is 'Not-I'. In Chapter 7, we describe how we make sense of something fully only in its context. A drop of water is understood very differently when it is perceived falling with many others as rain on the earth, or leaking from a pipe and dripping onto the carpet. It cannot be defined as an individual drop at all when it is part of a bath. Therefore 'I' can only be completely 'I', and know myself as 'I', when I am in relationship to something or someone else.

Strategic Relating and Authentic Relating

Sometimes we see the world and the people in it in terms of what we could do with them or what they might do with us. We think 'about' things and people: "The windows are dirty, shall I clean them?"; "There's John. He looks grumpy as usual." Even when we are talking to someone — "Hi, John, would you like some tea? It might cheer you up" — we are what is called 'manipulating our environment'. We make decisions about what people are like on the basis of our past experiences or our current wants and fantasies. Bob Resnick (personal communication, 1992) calls this 'strategic relating'. We use our previous experiences of life to understand a present situation and make predictions about it. Then, often out-of-awareness, we 'manipulate' the situation to bring about what we want or expect.

Consider two examples. In the first, a woman, whom I identify (using past experience — what else?) as my friend, approaches me, smiling. On the basis of my previous relationship with her, I assume that she has come for a chat. Quickly I put the kettle on, draw up two chairs and switch on the fire. Actually, she only popped over to borrow something but, faced with my setting of the chatting scene, she is easily attracted to stay. In the second example, I have been invited to a party and I feel nervous because I am afraid I will have nothing to say and everyone will think I am boring. It reminds me of countless times at school when I, an only child, felt an outsider and unaccepted by the group. I go to the party and because I am nervous I stand in the kitchen and talk to no-one. Almost inevitably no-one talks to me. I feel like a lonely outsider and am acutely aware of how boring I am being. In both examples, I have brought about the outcome I expected.

Sometimes, however, we see people in their *true* humanness rather than how they fit into our world, and we relate to them from *our* true humanness rather than from the image of ourselves that we want them to see. Bob Resnick called this 'authentic relating'. For example, a client finishes telling her counsellor about her agonizing dilemma: should she leave her husband or not? Despairingly, she appeals to him, "What should I do?" The counsellor resonates with her ambivalence and her despair. He answers, "I don't know." They look at each other in silence. They are two individuals sharing a moment of awareness of the complexity of life.

The Dialogue

In Gestalt this quality of meeting can be called an I–Thou dialogue. The concept originated with the work of the existentialist philosopher Martin Buber (1984) who struggled to identify what it was that caused people to grow and become the finest they could be. He decided (as others, such as Carl Rogers, have done) that the development of 'personhood' could only come out of an authentic meeting between two people who encounter each other as openly and non-defensively as they can, in the full awareness both of their individual separateness and of their connection. Personal growth and, according to Buber, even a spiritual transcendence occur between the people in that meeting.

Buber also talked about another form of relationship, which he referred to as I–It relating. In this form of relating we relate to the rest of the world (both people and things) as objects whose existence is for us to affect, control or manipulate. (Equally, we may feel as if 'It' affects, controls or manipulates us.) In ordinary living we must, of course, often relate to the world in this way in order to focus on our own needs, wants or plans. A frequent example is when we guess what a person is like (for instance, because of the way they look) and relate to them as if they were our image of them. This may be a correct image based on good observation or intuition, or it may be purely based on the fact that we expect the person to treat us in the way someone else has treated us — for instance our parents, teachers or friends. This is what is called transference, because we 'transfer' our experiences from the past into the present. In either case, it is I–It relating because it is based on our expectations rather than here and now experience.

We are very likely to adopt an I–It stance when the other person is in a particular role in relation to us, and we focus on the role instead of the person. For example, at a busy London station I may be very involved with the task of buying a ticket and getting to the right platform in time for my train. The gates are opening just as I arrive and a fairly large crowd starts surging down the ramp onto the platform. Bodies are crushed together in the press and everybody politely but firmly pushes forward to get a seat. We are in I–It mode, relating to the ticket-seller and the other travellers as stages in our task. This is not to say that we treat them rudely. On the contrary, we probably deal with them in the civil and pleasant manner with which we have learned to relate to people in the world when we are seeking a particular outcome: there will be many an "excuse me" and "thank you"; we do not shout or hit each other. Suddenly, I drop my umbrella and the woman next to me picks it up. As she gives it to me I meet her eyes and see a woman of about my age. I smile a thank you and she smiles back with real warmth. In that moment, I see the person behind the role of fellow passenger. We have a trivial exchange of words about the business of the train, yet we are both aware that we are having a real meeting. The relationship has become I–Thou. There is a qualitative difference in our encounter, brought about by that awareness of being two human beings in the world.

A life lived without the meeting of person to person would be sterile and, according to Buber, could not truly give us a sense of our real selves. Lynne Jacobs (1989) says, 'The I–It mode is vitally necessary for living, the I–Thou for the realisation of personhood', and quotes Buber as saying: 'Without It a human being cannot live but whoever lives with only that is not human.' We all need to spend much of our time in the I–It mode of relating to organize our lives. In describing the counselling relationship, Jacobs uses the term 'dialogic process' to refer to the essential movement between the counsellor's two modes of relating. The counselling relationship offers a special opportunity to engage with another human being in the I–Thou relationship in order to become our fullest selves.

Clearly, the counselling situation is a very particular form of meeting. Though the personal growth of both counsellor and client is possible, we must be aware that our clients are not there for *our* growth. We are both there with an agreed focus: the growth and development of the client. Our satisfaction must come from commitment to this task. In this sense, therefore, there is not a mutuality within the relationship. Here is an interesting paradox. We have said that, in terms of intention, there is not mutuality. This means that, in the wider context of the counselling situation, the relationship must be I–It. But this does not prevent a very real meeting from taking place. Within the counselling relationship, the counsellor holds a continuum between I–It and I–Thou. It is our task to approach clients with an I–Thou *attitude* or *intention*. We believe also that the client's growth involves developing the capacity for a fully mutual relationship.

Clients coming into counselling are unlikely to engage in an I–Thou relationship immediately. Most will be coming to see a counsellor at a time of difficulty or distress. They will see their counsellor perhaps as a potential problem solver, or even a 'magician' who will make them feel better. Some may rarely have had the experience of being fully aware of themselves in the present moment. Even those who have frequently had such experiences are likely to approach the counsellor at first from an I–It position. This is only natural and applies also to the counsellor. Before meeting, both will have created images, fantasies and expectations regarding each other based on past experiences. Importantly, the counsellor will bracket (see Chapter 9) these preconceptions, referring to them only in the service of understanding the client. As soon as they meet, he will make himself available to engage with the client in an I–Thou attitude. It is a counsellor's task at this point to facilitate the client in developing his here-and-now awareness. The client, naturally, will take time to adjust to the new room and the new situation, gradually moving from an I–It relationship to more frequent moments of I–Thou dialogue. This may happen in the first session, but some clients will take longer — weeks, or even months or years.

To reiterate, we are not suggesting that the counsellor will never use an I–It way of relating to her client. On the contrary, counsellors will use the I–It mode much of the time. To be constantly in I–Thou mode would not only be impossible but would mean that we never *thought* about our clients. Outside the session, we may think about the meaning of what the client has said and decide about what we want to take to our supervision (see Chapter 15); or we may use some strategic thinking in assessing what the client may need from us. In addition, it is part of a counsellor's job to use her clinical knowledge and experience within the session. For instance, if the client says he feels dreadfully depressed and cannot sleep, the counsellor may be aware of a moment of anxiety and particular concern. A 'priority' figure emerges: "Could this client be so severely depressed as to need medical help; could he even be a danger to himself?" It is important to find out what other 'symptoms' there are. The counsellor approaches the client with the express strategic plan of clarifying her judgement. For this period, the counsellor is inevitably relating in an I–It way, as she is not simply giving herself to the emerging moment, she is steering the conversation.

In Part III of this book, we describe a variety of techniques or ways of thinking about and using Gestalt theory. In order to facilitate their effective use, we have to be relating in an I–It way. However, the counsellor's intention is always that these interventions will arise out of having been in real dialogue with the client, and never just 'applied'.

Chapter 4

AWARENESS

Awareness is at the heart of both the theory and the practice of Gestalt counselling. Gary Yontef (Yontef & Simkin, 1989, p337) says: 'In Gestalt therapy, *the only goal is awareness*' (emphasis in original). Awareness is the full recognition of our experience. We are aware of what we are feeling, thinking and doing in the present moment and what is happening around us as it is happening. Again to quote the words of Gary Yontef, 'Awareness is a form of experience that may be loosely defined as being in touch with one's own existence, with *what is*' (*ibid*, emphasis in original). Put like this, it sounds obvious and not particularly extraordinary. How then can it be the heart of Gestalt?

In the following pages we will expand upon this deceptively simple concept of awareness and offer the reader an opportunity to recognize how very little we are aware in our normal day-to-day living and how enriching an increase in awareness can be. Being fully aware of ourselves means that we know ourselves and live our lives in a richer way. Being aware means being in the present, which by definition is new every moment. Experiences and perceptions are more vivid and powerful. Interactions which may have become semi-ritualized through habit take on a newness and immediacy. We are in touch with ourselves and the reality of the world around us.

Being aware also includes reclaiming qualities or aspects of ourselves which we have lost through disuse (such as intuition) or repression (such as feelings or thoughts which seemed unacceptable). There are many reasons why we disown parts of ourselves, some of which we discuss later in this book. Often this disowning is an 'unconscious' process, which means it is not made in awareness. Counselling can help people to reverse the disowning. As Erving and Miriam Polster (1973) put it, 'we . . .

try to bring into awareness that self which has been "betrayed" '.

Perls disagreed with Freud that the way to work with 'neuroses' (disturbances in healthy processes) was to trace them to their historical roots. Perls said that the only way really to experience life is in the present. Therefore, if we become aware of the way we operate in the present, including our neuroses, we will have the living process in the room, where we can take responsibility for what we are doing, become aware of our needs and restore choice to our lives. When our awareness is fully in the present, we have the potential to deal effectively with situations as they occur, rather than according to old habits which may not be meeting our needs.

There are three zones of awareness:

1 *The inner zone:* awareness of the body, bodily sensations of all kinds, proprioceptions and feelings. These aspects overlap and interrelate but we will be addressing them individually in order to heighten awareness of the richness of our inner world.

2 *The outer zone:* awareness through the five senses and also through talking and moving. Gestaltists call these the 'contact functions' as, in order to make contact fully with someone or something, we need to look, listen, see, hear, talk, touch, move, taste and smell.

3 *The middle zone:* awareness of fantasies, thoughts and imaginings. This, of course, is actually part of our inner world, but Fritz Perls called it the middle zone to highlight that one of its roles is to mediate between the inner and the outer zones — making sense of each. The middle zone, therefore, is vitally important to us. It is more highly developed than in any other mammal. It can be enormously creative and inventive. Yet it can be the source of problems. Perls believed that many of life's difficulties were caused by people living too much in the middle zone of remembering, imagining, dreaming and rationalizing. Remember that he exhorted us to 'lose our minds and come to our senses', evoking the inner and outer zones. In our work with clients, inviting them to raise the awareness of these two zones and experience them fully is crucial. However, helping them to become aware of the limitations and distortions of their middle zone and to harness the creativity and ingenuity of that zone is also a significant part of Gestalt counselling.

But enough of *talking* about these zones: we invite you to learn by *experience* as we take you on an exploration of your awareness zones.

Awareness of the Inner Zone

●

The Physical

Take a few moments to become aware of the position of your body at this moment. You may be sitting in a comfortable chair or at a table. You may be lying down or even standing up. Notice which parts of your body are relaxed and which are tense. Notice if there are areas of discomfort of which you had not been aware. One of your legs may be a little stiff, your back may be sore, you may even realize that you have a full bladder (in which case, do attend to this need — or any other distracting need that you notice). Move your shoulders a little and notice how your muscles in this area feel different. Are any other parts of your body affected by the movement? Stretch an arm or a leg and again notice the changes in your bodily sensations.

Find a comfortable place where you can sit or lie down and be undisturbed for a few minutes. Close your eyes and first of all concentrate on your breathing and the rise and fall of your chest and stomach as they expand to fill with air. Now slowly exhale. Breathe deeply and slowly a few times and then be aware of settling into a rhythm of breathing that is comfortable and right for you. Then focus your awareness on your right foot; be aware of its shape and solidity. As you breathe in, tense the muscles in your toes and foot, then, as you breathe out, let your muscles relax and let the tension flow out. Become aware of your right calf. Again, tighten the muscles in it as you breathe in and relax them as you breathe out. Do the same for your knee, your thigh and your buttock. Do the same for your other leg. Then continue the process slowly around your body — your back, your genitals, your stomach, your chest, your shoulders, arms, hands, neck and head. Pay special attention as you become aware of your head — the back of your neck, the top of your head — and then each part of your face — your forehead, eyes, nose, cheeks, lips, tongue, chin. Try to caress the inside of your body with your awareness. See if you can become aware of your heart beating and your digestive organs working. Focus again on your breathing and stay aware of your whole body. If you become aware of passing thoughts or external distractions, simply notice them and let them go. Continue to sit or lie in that state of relaxed awareness for a few minutes.

You can, if you wish, do this exercise with a partner talking you slowly through the stages. Or you could dictate it onto a tape recorder, speaking very slowly and calmly, and perhaps adding extra phrases that have particular meaning for you. Then play it to yourself.

Feelings and Emotions

You may already have become aware of your emotions during the last exercise as they are, of course, intrinsically bound up in your body. Often people report having different feelings in different parts of their bodies. Some people who are not accustomed to recognizing their feelings also, not surprisingly, have difficulty in recognizing the bodily sensations to which they are connected. They may need help in naming feelings that they have and using them as a signal to themselves about their experience.

How are you feeling now? Notice what you do in order to find out what you are feeling, how you turn your awareness to yourself, what you use as indicators. You may not be feeling a strong feeling, but you will be feeling something, some version or combination of the four basic feelings of happiness, sadness, anger and fear — although you may not use those names. Usually we use words like OK, fed up, bored, anxious, depressed and so on. There are countless nuances of feeling. For simplicity, we invite you to explore your experience of the basic ones.

HAPPINESS

Remember a time when you felt really happy. Try to recapture that experience in the present. Be aware of how your body feels when you are happy: you may feel tingling energy in your limbs, your face may be alert, you may want to smile.

SADNESS

Now remember a time of sadness. Do you feel heavy in your chest or stomach or face, a prickling behind your eyes?

ANGER

Now remember the last time you were angry. What were you angry about? How do you know when you are angry? Your shoulders, arms and hands may get tense as if you were ready for a fight. You may feel your face get hot and your jaw tense.

FEAR

Think of something of which you are frightened. Where do you feel fear? Often people feel it as a leaden tension in the stomach, or a fluttering in the chest. You may feel short of breath and you may be aware of the blood draining from your face. Your eyes may widen.

Strong feelings, when part of a 'here and now' experience, are often noisy and wet. We shout, we cry, we scream, we laugh. We express them quite naturally and they finish quite soon. In a continuing situation like a bereavement, the feelings finish after they are expressed but come again, in waves. Less strong feelings have similar patterns, although they may be less noisy. Sometimes, however, we get into a feeling 'habit' where we may repeatedly repress our feeling or express a familiar feeling rather than respond freshly to an experience. Towards the end of Chapter 6 we talk about these habituated responses in more detail as 'fixed gestalts'.

Now imagine that you are stuck in a traffic jam on your way to the station. Your train leaves in 20 minutes and you are crawling along at a snail's pace. What are you feeling? Where in your body? Is this a familiar feeling for you at times of difficulty or stress?

AROUSED CURIOSITY

There is some debate about whether curiosity is one of the natural feelings. We believe strongly that it is a drive with which we are born. We have only to watch the activities of a baby to see how innate is the desire to reach out, to explore the world and how each new discovery is greeted with wonder. It is curiosity which stimulates the infant to learn to crawl as they spot an attractive new object and mobilize themselves to go towards it.

When did you last feel curious about something? What bodily sensations went with that curiosity? Try and re-experience them a little now. Do you feel an arousal of excitement in your chest or your stomach? Do you feel energy in your limbs? Your breath may quicken and your heart beat faster.

Awareness of the Middle Zone

In this area of our inner world are words and images as well as fully formed thoughts. Again take a few minutes to sit comfortably. Close your eyes if you wish. Let yourself be aware of any thoughts, memories or fantasies that you have. Try not to get 'attached' to any of them. Simply notice them and let them go. Do not force them or shape them. Do not censor them or, if you do, just be aware of that, too, and move on. You may find it interesting to speak your thoughts onto a tape recorder so that you can listen to them later. Notice how many of your thoughts are memories, or plans for the future, rather than fresh awareness in the here and now. These of course are part of, and necessary to, our everyday living but we can sometimes be astonished at how little of our thinking is truly a response to the present moment.

Like feelings, sometimes our thoughts become habituated. Are you aware of recurring themes in your thoughts? Return to the fantasy about being stuck in the traffic jam. Along with your feelings, are you aware of any thoughts or images associated with the scene, such as "I'm so stupid, I should have left earlier" or "Why does this always happen to me?" or "I'm going to be in trouble with the boss"? Are any of these thoughts familiar in times of difficulty? If so, they may be part of the habitual responses or fixed gestalts that we mentioned earlier.

Awareness of the Outer Zone

●

We are asking you to do the following five exercises as you sit where you are now. However, we invite you to do them regularly in a variety of situations and settings — on the underground, in the park, watching television, standing in the bus queue, in the office and so on. Notice how your experience of the present moment changes when you do this.

Seeing

Look up from this book. What do you see? Notice the shapes of the things or people around you. Notice their colour and size, their distance and closeness, whether their outlines and details are clear or indistinct. If you are in a room, look at the corners. Do you notice any cobwebs or marks which you have not noticed before? Now look at your hands. Really study the shape, the lines, any hairs, scars, freckles or veins. We often talk of knowing something 'like the back of our hands'. If you had no identifying accessories like nail varnish or rings, are you sure that you would be able to recognize your hand amongst a lot of other hands?

Listening

You might find it useful to close your eyes for this exercise. Pay attention to what you hear. Notice differences in pitch, volume, tone and intensity. Can you tell the proximity of the sounds? Is it a quiet sound close to you or a loud sound far away? Can you hear the sound of your breathing? You will notice that there are many sounds of which you were not previously aware or which you had incorporated into the background. There may be the sound of birds or of traffic or the hum of machinery. If we let ourselves be aware of all the noises in our life, it would be difficult to concentrate on anything else.

Touching

Get up and move around your environment, touching and feeling the different objects around you. Notice whether they are hot or cold, rough or smooth, angular or rounded. With your eyes closed, pick up an object and feel it all over. Try to do this as if you had no knowledge of what the object is and as if you are exploring it for the first time. Notice how sensitive you are and how much information you get from your fingers. Now explore your left hand with your right hand and be aware of the sensations in both. Put both your hands up to the top of your head and gently massage your scalp. Again, notice the sensation in your fingers and also the effect on your head.

Practise whole body awareness. Notice the places where your body meets the environment. Feel the pressure of the chair under you, and your feet on the floor. Notice if there are any draughts or wind and the way your skin feels. Do you feel warm or cool?

Tasting

If you are near a kitchen, fetch a small thing to eat, like a raisin, a piece of cheese or bread. Sit down and close your eyes. Put the morsel in your mouth and very slowly begin to eat it. Notice how your salivary glands begin to work and how the texture of the food changes in your mouth. Is it crunchy and rough or smooth and slippery? Notice whether you prefer to chew or to suck and pay minute attention as your taste buds respond. Is the food bitter or sweet, salty or bland? Does the taste change in any way? Let yourself be aware if you feel the urge to swallow quickly and resist it for a few moments. Then, when you are completely ready, swallow and feel the food as it goes down your throat into your stomach. How often do you take the time really to make contact with your food like this? Probably, like us, you usually eat with much of your awareness involved elsewhere. By paying attention to what you put into your body in this way, you can transform your eating habits. You may also think that it is a respectful way to treat your body!

Smelling

Move around your environment, picking things up and smelling them. You may be surprised how many things have a smell. Particularly if you are near a garden or a kitchen, notice all the many different smells there. Smell a jar of coffee, an orange, a loaf of bread, different plants. Be aware of whether the smells are sharp and pungent or sweet and perfumed, stale and musty or fresh and clear. Lick the back of your hand and then smell it. Notice the scent of your own skin.

Talking

Experiment with finding seven different ways to say: "I have a suggestion for you." Try varying the pitch, the tone, the intonation of your voice; try whispering; try projecting from your belly to the back of the proverbial lecture hall.

Moving

This time imagine that you have a client sitting opposite you and find seven different ways of conveying a message or impression to the client by the way you are sitting in your chair. Use body posture, position, angle, muscle tone, facial expression and so on.

Finally, allow yourself to be aware of *all* your senses. There are no rules and there is no 'right' way of doing this. Simply be aware of the sights, sounds, textures, smells, tastes and motions you are experiencing at this moment. Allow your awareness to flow between your senses.

PRACTICE WITH A PARTNER

Ask a friend or colleague to do this exercise with you. Start by observing each other and take it in turns to speak. Do not interpret what you notice. Simply state what you see: "I am aware of the collar of your jacket as it curves over your neck. I am aware of your eyes as you look at me and I notice how blue they are. Now I am noticing you smiling and looking away from me. I am aware of the little lines at the side of your mouth and now I am noticing how your body is curled in the chair", and so on. Then focus on what your partner is saying. Notice the sound of their voice and the words they are using: "I am aware of you speaking quite fast. I am aware of you noticing more about my face than my body. I am aware of you noticing colours and I am now aware that your voice is soft", and so on. You may find this exercise surprisingly intimate and yet all you are doing is bringing to your awareness, and verbalizing, some of the many things we may, in our day-to-day lives, take for granted. Explore by touch each other's hands and be aware of yourself as giver and receiver. Gently massage each other's shoulders and again be aware of your experience.

Combining the Zones

You can use this exercise in order to observe and enhance the natural flow of your moment-by-moment awareness. Find a comfortable place to sit and let yourself monitor the focus of your awareness as it changes and shifts. Use the introduction, "Now I am aware ..." to describe your experience. Do not forget that there is no right or wrong way of doing this exercise: your experience is your experience. Simply notice whatever you are aware of and move on without criticism or judgement of yourself. If you find yourself being distracted from the exercise, just notice that too. For example, "Now I am aware of a wisp of cloud above a tree-top. Now I am aware of wondering if it is going to rain. Now I am aware of remembering the washing hanging on the line. Now I am aware of my teeth pressing together. Now I am aware that I am cold. Now I am aware of feeling amused at doing this exercise", and so on.

Do the exercise again for a few minutes. This time use a tape-recorder or, better still, a partner. You will notice quite a different quality in the exercise if someone else is present. Use the partner or the tape-recorder to get feedback about your own awareness. Notice which types of awareness are most strong or frequent for you. Do you spend more time in your inner zone, your middle or your outer zone? Which of your senses do you use most? Is your inner awareness of bodily sensations, thoughts or feelings? Again, you may notice that it is quite hard to stay fully aware in the present moment, especially if you are doing the exercise on your own. You may find that you have followed some train of thought and forgotten to be aware for some time. If this happens, do not worry, just notice when you become aware again and move on. Similarly, you may find yourself unaccountably wanting to stop the exercise or censor some of your awareness. Just notice this also — "I am aware of avoiding something" — and stay with your experience.

Here is an exercise in structuring your awareness. Take it in stages. Start with noticing something in your outer zone and then move to the inner or middle zone for your next awareness. Use the format, "I see/hear/smell/etc . . . and I feel [this may be a sensation or emotion] . . . and I think . . .". For example, "I see the poster for the fair and I feel excited and I think I will take a friend to the fair" or "I hear a clinking in the street and I think that it is probably the milkman . . . I think about breakfast and I feel hungry."

Now do this exercise with a partner. For instance, "I see you raise your eyebrows and I think you are expecting something from me and I feel anxious as I think I don't know what you want . . . I notice you are leaning forward now and I feel warm towards you and I think you like me . . . I hear you laugh and I feel happy and I think I am enjoying doing this exercise with you." Be aware of how you make meaning of your experiences. This is the work of the middle zone. In discussing the exercise afterwards with your partner, you may discover not only that you have a propensity to notice particular things but that there are certain themes to your meaning making. In Part III of this book, we will look at ways in which awareness of this kind can be helpful to your clients.

Our last exercise focuses on another important element of awareness: those things of which we choose to remain unaware. Again, do this exercise by yourself and then with a friend. Become aware of your experiences as before, but this time say, "I am aware of . . . and what I left out was . . .". You may even experiment with saying, "I am aware that I am avoiding notic- ing . . .". You may be surprised at what you notice now that you have brought other elements into your awareness.

Reflections on Awareness

●

If you did some or all of the previous exercises, you may have no- ticed the following features of awareness:

1 Awareness is *here* — at this place, and *now* — at this time. We can only be aware in the present moment. Even if we are recalling the past or anticipating the future we cannot fully experience them; we can only have memories or fantasies which are part of our present awareness. Thus we can use thoughts and images to dwell upon the past or the future. Aware experience can only be in the present.

2 The flow of awareness is uneven. We move our attention from element to element and from zone to zone, sometimes in a flow of associations, sometimes in response to sudden distractions and changes in stimuli.

3 There are many areas of awareness and many channels through which we become aware. They can be divided into awareness of the external world (the outer zone) and our internal world (the inner zone and the middle zone). Awareness of contact between our inner and outer worlds leads to increased knowledge of who and how we are and greater vividness of experience.

4 Potentially, there are innumerable elements of which we can become aware at any one moment. We may have a general, wide-ranging awareness of several of these elements or we may focus more sharply upon one element. If we are really focusing our attention, it is impossible to be fully aware of more than one thing at a time. Try focusing on this book and also on how you are feeling at the same time. Difficult isn't it? You will notice that what actually happens is that your awareness flickers back and forth between the two. We organize the many stimuli in our world into what in Gestalt are called 'figures', allowing the rest to become 'ground'. So a figure is where we are focusing our awareness and the ground involves all else. Which figures we choose to focus upon can have relevance in counselling. For instance, our client may choose to make figure the fact that Mary did not smile at him rather than the fact that John did. Healthy living lies in making 'lively' figures and being aware of the choices we are making in doing so. We will come back to this important concept in subsequent chapters.

5 As we become aware of different elements in our world, we organize them into whole figures and make meaning out of them. It is important to be aware of the meanings we are making in order to widen our options of choice. For instance, when Jo frowned, Bob thought that meant she was thinking something through, while Tim thought that she was angry.

We end this chapter with three quotations. They complement each other in their acknowledgement of the importance of aware-ness. The first is a definition from Yontef & Simkin (1989) who say: 'Full awareness is the process of being in vigilant contact with the most important events in the individual/environmental field, with full sensory-motor, emotional, cognitive and energetic support.' The second is an expression of awe: 'Awareness is huge. It's like asking, "What is a person?" "What is the meaning of life?"' (Joseph Zinker, 1990). The third is a celebration by Henry Miller, cited by David Schiller in *The Little Zen Companion* (1994): 'The aim of life is to live, and to live is to be aware — joyously, drunkenly, serenely, divinely aware.'

Chapter 5

CONCEPTS OF HEALTH AND ILL-HEALTH IN GESTALT

Health

In general terms, healthy people think and feel positively about themselves a lot of the time. They have satisfying relationships and find ways of using their life in satisfying and creative ways. They are actively involved with other people and the environment, relating rather than reacting, aware of their needs and taking responsibility for meeting those needs creatively and constructively while remaining aware and respectful of others and the environment.

Part of being healthy is the ability to self-regulate and self-support in times of stress as well as to recognize the need for the support of others. This means the development of mutually interdependent relationships as opposed to dependent or exploitative ones. Healthy people also take responsibility for the choices they make in life and for the meaning they make of their lives. Awareness of themselves and their environment is intrinsic to this responsibility. Healthy people experience themselves and the world and make appropriate and creative adjustments informed by their awareness.

As you will see as you read this book, awareness is not a laborious process of perpetual or obsessional navel-gazing. The Gestalt view of healthy awareness places emphasis on immediacy of contact with others and the environment without the 'baggage' of the past or the future. Healthy people have the capacity to live fully in the here and now with all the aliveness and vibrancy that implies. This does not mean being happy all the time but being alive and in contact with others and the environment with a whole range of feelings, thoughts and actions. A healthy person feels sad, angry, excited or scared and fully expresses those feelings in appropriate ways.

In his book, *Creative Process in Gestalt Therapy* (1977), Joseph Zinker suggests that, in the course of counselling, a person:

▶ moves toward greater awareness of himself — his body, his feelings, his environment;

▶ learns to take ownership of his experiences, rather than projecting them onto others;

▶ learns to be aware of his needs and to develop skills to satisfy himself without violating others;

▶ moves toward a fuller contact with his sensations, learning to smell, taste, touch, hear and see to savour all aspects of himself;

▶ moves toward the experience of his power and the ability to support himself, rather than relying on whining, blaming or guilt-making in order to mobilise support from the environment;

▶ becomes sensitive to his surroundings, yet at the same time wears a coat of armour for situations which are potentially destructive or poisonous;

▶ learns to take responsibility for his actions and their consequences;

▶ feels comfortable with the awareness of his fantasy life and its expression.

Naranjo (1970) gives a list of healthy injunctions regarding desirable ways of experiencing. Therapeutic activities in Gestalt are based upon these values.

1 Live in the 'now'.

2 Live in the 'here', in the immediate situation.

3 Accept yourselves as you are.

4 See your environment and interact with it as it is, not as you wish it to be.

5 Be honest with yourselves.

6 Express yourselves in terms of·what you want, think, feel, rather than manipulate self and others through rationalizations, expectations, judgements and distortions.

7 Experience fully the complete range of emotions, the unpleasant as well as pleasant.

8 Accept no external demands that go contrary to your best knowledge of yourself.

9 Be willing to experiment, to encounter new situations.

10 Be open to change and growth.

All the above aspects of health are ideals. They are what a person may aspire towards in their life. In this sense, health is a process of development towards these ideals — a continuing process, not just throughout counselling but throughout life. As in life, counselling is usually a cyclical or spiralling rather than a linear process, coming back to the same issues perhaps, but at a different level or angle in order to enhance our experience.

Ill-health

Perls pointed out that we all have disturbances of one form or another which may block our achievement of these ideals. Gestalt counselling directly addresses these disturbances as we move towards our objective of psychological health. Here we consider some of the common patterns which prevent us from living our life to the full.

We may be overdependent upon environmental support. This means that we may rely on others to the extent that we are passive and undirected, waiting for them to look after us or to tell us what to do. Dependence usually leads to our adapting to others' demands without reference to our own feelings, beliefs or wants. Alternatively, we may live in an overindependent way, rebelling against the demands of others or refusing to participate in the 'give-and-take' of relationships.

We may limit our range of experiences by suppressing our sensations, feelings or thoughts so that we are out of contact with our real selves.

We may disown parts of ourselves by clinging to a specific self-image. A concept from Eastern philosophy is that of the yin and the yang: two opposite types of energy, the two sides to each situation or state of being. The word in Gestalt which describes this concept is 'polarities'. Every quality has its opposite quality. Sometimes, however, we are attached to the idea of ourselves as being a particular way, for example calm, kind or gentle. We are unwilling to 'own' the inevitable 'other side of the coin' which may be boisterous, selfish or rough.

We may be either stuck at one end of a polarity or constantly swinging to extremes without the subtle gradations of experience in between. Thus we miss the 'point of creative indifference' (Friedländer, 1918): the mid-point between the polarities when we approach the world without investment or prejudice, open to any experience and any possibility. Figure 1 depicts polarities first as a line with opposite extremes and secondly as a circle with the two polarities very near each other. The latter illustrates the phenomenon of the violent switch from one polarity to another when suddenly they do not seem far apart (as in the benign person who rarely gets angry but becomes aggressive when he does).

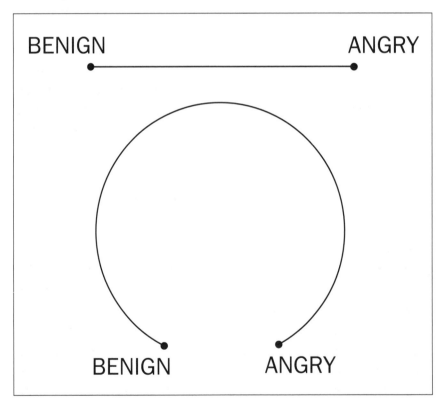

Figure 1   *Polarities*

We may be acting from habit, unaware of the options we have in any given situation. We react to the world from fixed patterns of perception and behaviour based on expectations formed in past experiences. Our relationships, instead of being grounded in the honest exchange of thoughts, feelings and wants, are distorted by prejudices, hopes and old beliefs. (Incidentally, Hunter Beaumont — personal communication 1992 — suggests that what we call 'character' is actually the collection of fixed patterns of thinking, feeling and behaving that we have developed throughout our lives.)

We may be 'acting out' our lives rather than living them, spending a lot of energy outside the here and now, dwelling on, or even psychologically in, the past or the future. At any given moment we may be concentrating, not on what is happening to us in the present, but on memories of what has passed or on concerns for what may be going to happen. Or we may be saying, "I wonder what Jim is doing now," focusing on the 'there' rather than on our own surroundings, the 'here'.

We may reject who we are and strive constantly to be somebody else.

We may cling to the familiar and smother our natural drive for growth.

If we do these things, we are not in good contact with ourselves, others or the environment; the present becomes a misty place devoid of clear figures and the excitement of the moment.

Self and Environment

Many people familiar with the Gestalt of the 1960s and 1970s were put off by the seemingly individualistic view of health summed up as 'Do your own thing'. Maybe this was a necessary swing towards individuality at the time. Maybe it was a gross misunderstanding of the Gestalt approach. Either way, since those early days, there has been an increasing emphasis on awareness not just of the individual but of the environmental field within which the individual exists — and without which they cannot exist. Emphasis is placed upon the interconnectedness of individuals with their surroundings. Awareness of context, and responsibility within that context, are as much a part of the healthy ideal as our personal intrapsychic processes. Our relationships with others, our friends and families, the local community, the wider community, the global community as well as our relationship to the physical world and its resources, especially in our times of horrors such as atmospheric pollution and deforestation, can no longer be ignored as irrelevant or outside our responsibility. Health includes all this. Absence of such an awareness suggests some degree of ill-health.

These ideas for living well are not new. The following guidelines come from the Native American Indians:

▶ Treat the earth and all that dwell thereon with respect.
▶ Show great respect for your fellow beings.
▶ Work together for the benefit of all mankind.
▶ Give assistance and kindness wherever needed.
▶ Look after the well-being of mind and body.
▶ Dedicate a share of your efforts to the greater good.
▶ Be truthful and honest at all times.
▶ Take full responsibility for your actions.

Summary
●

Health is the natural state to which we are born. Consider a healthy young child: aware, lively, flexible, creative, adaptable, responsible, relational. Ill-health is any interruption, disturbance or rigidity in these qualities. We can describe it in many ways, but ultimately the best definition is that this is what our clients bring us in the form of their distress.

Chapter 6

THE FORMATION AND COMPLETION OF GESTALTS

Wholeness

As we said in Chapter 1, the word 'gestalt' comes from the German and translates as 'an organized whole'. It means that the wholeness of something — an object, an idea, a situation or a person — is not only more than the sum of its parts but also different from those parts.

As you are reading this book, you are forming gestalts or wholes. Each word is made up of letters but, unless you are just learning to read or are unfamiliar with a particular word, you will not be sounding out each letter but allowing your eyes to take in each word as a whole. It is the whole from which we make meaning. The parts, the individual letters, represent only single sounds. For example, the letters S, N, O, W taken by themselves are written symbols of particular sounds and have no meaning for us beyond that. However, if we see them together in this order *as a whole*, they instantly have meaning for us. Change the order to OWNS, and, though the parts remain the same, a new whole is formed and a totally different meaning is derived from the change in their organization. The same is true of phrases or sentences. The parts, now the individual words, are again less than and different from the meaning of the sentence. If words are added, deleted or merely reorganized, the meaning of the whole phrase or sentence is changed. 'The snow was falling onto the house' is very different from 'the house was falling onto the snow'.

But there is a wider context, a greater whole, in the process of reading and understanding words. We may form the letters S, N, O, W into the word SNOW but, without some knowledge or experience of what snow is, we are left with a collection of sounds.

We need some prior experience of a particular sound and a symbolic connection that we can make in order to make the word meaningful. The French words *la neige* will have no meaning for us unless we can translate the words into our own language and have a general knowledge or experience of snow. Our understanding of the words, the whole, is dependent upon our experience. One person's experience may be very different from another's so we cannot assume, even with words, that we are making the same meaning. Someone from the tropics whose knowledge of snow has been gained purely through descriptions and photographs will have a very different perception of snow from that of an Eskimo.

The importance of wholeness to the counsellor is wide. First, it has an impact on the way we approach the client. We see them 'holistically' as a complete person: body, mind and soul. We do not just look at one problematical aspect of them. We also see them within their context as a whole, taking into account the cultural and socioeconomic circumstances in which they live, and significant events which are affecting their lives. For instance, a woman comes to see a counsellor because she is depressed. The counsellor does not simply think, "Here is a person who is depressing her emotions." The whole picture is explored. Has the woman been depressed before; is it a common feeling for her? Has she recently suffered a bereavement or other major change? Has she had a baby? How is her physical health? How is her social network? And so on.

The second significant impact of wholeness is on the way we use the concept in the here and now meeting with the client. The way they constellate their world — the 'wholes' of meaning that they make, the gestalts they see and create in their lives — is *who they are*. The counsellor's aim is to create a relationship with the client (to co-create a gestalt) in which they can become aware of how they constellate their world. In the following sections, we explore the most important elements of wholeness and what they mean for us as human beings.

Figure and Ground

●

While you are reading this book, you are paying visual attention to the words on the page as well as making meaning of those words. Peripherally, you may visually perceive what is below, above and to the sides of the book: maybe the colour and pattern of your clothes below, the surface of a table to the sides and the sunlight from a window over the top of the book, depending upon the environmental context of your reading. The book is figure, the room and objects within it are ground. Momentarily, you may look up as someone passes by the window and your constellation of figure and ground changes. The person becomes figure and the book joins the other aspects in becoming ground. Take a look at the picture below:

Did you see a Madonna and Child? Half close your eyes and look again at the area where the mother's left hand comes round the child's body. You may see a face which is much less appealing. You will notice that, when you see the ugly head, you cannot see the hand and the fold of cloth. The rest of the picture becomes ground. If you focus again on the mother and child, the picture resumes its beauty.

Similarly, Perls, Hefferline and Goodman, drawing upon the work of the Gestalt psychologists mentioned earlier, used a now well known diagram (Figure 2, opposite) to illustrate the same point. If you see the black parts as the ground and the white as figure, you will perceive a white chalice. If you see the white part as ground and the black as figure, you will perceive the silhouettes of two faces in profile facing each other. Although it is possible to shift your attention very quickly from one to the other, you cannot see both simultaneously. As soon as you make one figure, the other becomes ground. But notice too that the figure and the ground are mutually dependent. You cannot see the chalice without the ground of the faces and vice versa. Both are necessary in order to perceive the figure within the ground. Thus, as we will go on to discuss later under field-theory, everything has importance and relevance: there is a connectedness within the whole.

Gestaltists use the concept of figure and ground to explain the process by which human beings organize their perceptions to form wholes in order to create meaning. As with the picture of the faces and the chalice, we cannot see the totality of ourselves and our environment simultaneously. Some things become figure while others remain ground, depending upon our needs at the time. This can be illustrated with the simple example of post-boxes. In going about our everyday business, we do not usually notice post-boxes, but if we urgently need to post a letter, we start to search for one. For this short time, a post-box becomes figure against the ground of everything else. Once the letter is posted, post-boxes again recede into the ground of our perception.

We will expand upon connectedness in Chapter 7, but for the time being, as it is so intrinsic to figure and ground, this is a good place to continue using the post-box example. We can see that our need to send a letter must be connected to our knowledge and experience that letters are put into post-boxes, that

Figure 2   *'Visuell wahrgenommene figuren' by Edgar Rubin,*
Gyldendalske Boghandel, Copenhagen, 1921

post-boxes are found in certain places, that for the most part
they are a certain shape and a certain colour. Hence, perhaps,
our hesitation to post a letter in foreign countries, when faced
with a square, yellow construction with only a letter-shaped hole
to give some reassurance! The letter will need a stamp of a particular value and will be addressed to the person to whom we are
sending it. All of this may seem pretty obvious to us: we have

absorbed all the interconnected aspects of posting a letter into the ground of our awareness, so we need not bring them all fully into figure. Yet they are intrinsically part of the whole, leading towards the completion of that whole by the posting of the letter.

Completion

●

Not only do we have a natural tendency to see wholes, we also have an 'urge to complete'. We seek to make wholes and, therefore, meaning out of parts. Writing and reading are clearly skills which have to be learnt but they draw upon this natural human tendency towards completion. Even a child learning to read (unless they have some perceptual learning difficulties) will quite soon begin to constellate individual letters into words and make meaning of them without giving attention to the parts of which they are made up. Having read this chapter so far, it will be difficult for you to see the letters SNO without adding a W and completing the word.

This natural tendency for completion and the formation of wholes was demonstrated in the 1920s and 1930s by Gestalt psychologists experimenting with principles of perception. They would show their students a series of incomplete pictures consisting of lines and shapes which the students would make sense of by seeing them as complete pictures. You have probably done this many times yourself as you notice the 'doodle' you have drawn while talking on the telephone. You perceive these accidental lines, loops and shapes as a face, a flower or some animal. You visually 'fill in the gaps' to create a whole. You may even go on to complete them on the paper. The same is true of 'cloud-watching' where, in the masses, the swirls, the light and shade of the clouds you perceive a castle, a dragon, a landscape. An example of this phenomenon is provided by Figure 3, where there is a small collection of lines but you have no difficulty in perceiving a face.

Our tendency to complete and create wholes applies to our everyday lives, moment by moment, as well as over time. If a conversation with a friend is interrupted in the middle of an exciting tale, we will want to return to it as soon as possible to

Figure 3 *Completion*

hear the rest, to get the complete story. If we are reading a good
novel, we will find it difficult to put the book down (especially
nearing the end) without knowing how it ends. Novelists, play-
wrights and film-makers all capitalise upon our need to complete
and make wholes. The daily 'soap opera' in particular is
renowned for its 'cliff-hanger' endings each day which ensure a
good viewing audience for the next episode.

There may be certain tasks which, if they are incomplete, are
difficult to forget until they are completed. You may keep remembering the letter you need to post, the message you need to deliver, the laundry you need to finish, the book you need to take
back to the library, and so on. You find you cannot totally put
these thoughts aside until you have completed the tasks. Once
they are done, our attention can be devoted to other things more
clearly.

Similarly, this tendency for completion and wholeness applies
to our emotional lives. Jim, for example, has not seen or heard
from Stephanie for many years since she ended her relationship
with him to take up a job abroad. He felt very hurt but did not let
himself show it. He 'soldiered on' with his life, although feeling a

frequent sense of depression. However, on meeting her again when she returns to London, he immediately feels all the hurt and anger he had not allowed expression at the time. He feels he cannot relate to Stephanie until he has told her about his feelings: they seem to get in the way of his renewing their friendship. Once they have been shared and expressed — in other words, once completion of that particular emotional gestalt is achieved — he can relate to Stephanie more fully in the present.

Our life experience is full of gestalts, formed, completed and then formed again. It is possible to see this process of completion and formation as a cycle.

The Cycle of Experience as a Model of Healthy Functioning

In all aspects of life there are beginnings, middles and endings which can be seen as cyclical. There is the regular rhythm of night and day, waking and sleeping or breathing out and breathing in. There is the perpetual cycle of hunger for food and need for the satisfaction of that hunger and, of course, there is the life cycle itself from seed to birth, from early growth to maturity, from ageing to dying. In plants and animals, including human beings, the next generation continues the cycle of life. All living organisms can be seen to be moving through their life cycle and within that overall cycle through millions of sub-cycles along the way — each species at a different rate and level of complexity. In Gestalt we focus on the cycles of experience of which life is made.

Imagine someone is lying in bed asleep. The telephone rings. Through the mist of their dreamy sleep the sound of its bell begins to disturb them. As gradually they wake, they become aware of the insistent noise which for a few moments seemed to be part of their dream. They realize it is the telephone. For a few moments they lie still, wondering whether to answer it and, having decided to do so, they stretch their limbs before sitting up and reaching for the phone. They pick it up and say, "Hello" and a voice says, "Hi, you told me to wake you at seven-fifteen." The person thanks the caller, replaces the receiver and falls back onto the pillow. Their muscles relax again as they take some minutes to rest and gather their thoughts ready for the day.

We have just followed someone through one of the many natural cycles of which our lives are made. During the course of our lives we are subject to millions of stimuli which we automatically sort through and prioritize. These stimuli could be internal ones, such as a sensation of hunger, an emotion or a sudden idea, or they could be an external event, such as the telephone in our example, the sound of a voice, the action of another person or a change in the weather. Many of these stimuli remain part of the 'ground' and we do not make them part of our awareness. Many we notice briefly as transient 'figures'. Some we focus on and bring into our awareness as sharp 'figures'. In our example, the ringing telephone started in the ground or field of the slumbering dreamer. Gradually, it became figure and the person prepared to respond to it and take action. The phone was answered, the message received and the experience/gestalt was complete. The person was ready to focus on the new emerging figure, which was the plan for the day.

Gestalt counsellors believe that healthy functioning is this process of noticing, forming a figure and taking action, in awareness, in the present moment, taking responsibility for the choices we make both in the selection of figure and in our response to it.

The idea that there are stages to our experience was originally expressed by Perls (1947) and Paul Goodman (Perls *et al*, 1951) and developed by Zinker (1977). Under various titles it has been divided into several different stages by different theorists at different times which, in itself, reflects the growing and changing nature of Gestalt. We are presenting our version here which you may wish to compare and contrast with others (see Clarkson and Mackewn, 1993).

Stage 1: Sensation

The individual experiences a stimulus either from the environment or from within herself. This stage is called 'Sensation' because it involves the impact of the stimulus on our senses. For instance, something may pass across our visual field or we may begin to feel some bodily sensations. In our example, there is the external stimulus of the ringing sound of the telephone which the sleeper begins to hear.

Stage 2: Recognition

The sensation emerges as figure for the individual who becomes aware of it, locates it and attempts to recognize it and, if possible, name it. An internal sensation of tightness in the chest may be recognized immediately as sadness by a particular person, while for another it may be recognized as the beginnings of a cold. For yet another person, the recognition may not be so easily labelled and may remain simply as an awareness of tightness. In our example, the awakening is accompanied by the gradual identification of the sound as a telephone bell.

Stage 3: Appraisal and Planning (Mobilizing Energy)

At this stage the individual begins to respond to the stimulus, make sense of it and decide what to do. She feels and thinks about the sensation and experiences a rise in energy as she prepares to act. Sometimes this appraisal will assist in the recognition process as the individual reacts and responds to something new and unfamiliar. Sometimes it will be the increasing awareness of the person's need or feeling as she sorts through various options and chooses her plan of action. In our example, the person, having recognized the telephone, decides to answer it and readies her muscles for action.

Stage 4: Action

Now the individual makes some movement towards achieving her goal. She may experiment with different courses of action until she finds the satisfactory one, or there may only be one direction to take. The plan is put into action. For instance, the person rolls over and stretches out to reach the telephone.

Stage 5: Contact

Here the individual becomes fully engaged with whatever she has chosen to do. Everything else temporarily recedes into the background as the action meets the need and becomes a vivid and full figure. For instance, a hungry man savours his sandwich and, in that moment, that is his only involvement; a woman focuses all her senses on the sight and sound of bees as they alight on the pale, pink flowers. And in our example, the person lifts the receiver, hears her friend's voice and receives the message.

Stage 6: Assimilation and Completion

If the need has been fully met with full contact, the person feels a physiological and psychological sense of completion and satisfaction. Even if the action was the expression of sadness and weeping, some sense of relief and appropriateness will be experienced. At this stage, the person checks with herself to make sure that the need has been met, in a process which can also be called 'reappraisal'. If the original sensation and awareness remain, the person may return to the appraisal stage to form a new plan. In this way, we see how we may shuttle back and forth between the stages as we constantly respond with awareness to inner and outer stimuli in what Perls *et al* called 'organismic self-regulation' (1951) and Hunter Beaumont (1993) calls 'self-organization'.

In our example, the person has made complete sense of the morning's disturbance and is ready to let the experience go. The individual moves into the final stage.

Stage 7: Withdrawal

The individual withdraws her attention from this figure which now becomes ground as it gradually loses its interest. In our example, the person replaces the receiver and relaxes back onto the pillows, ready to turn her attention to other things. The gestalt is complete (see Figure 4).

The Space Between

There is a space between stages seven and one of the Gestalt cycle. It is not exactly a stage because, by definition, it is not a moving on. It is the state of being, after withdrawal but before the emergence of the next figure, during which a person is at rest. Perls (1976) referred to it as 'the fertile void'. Ideally, in this state, we do not fill our lives with memories and plans, but are willing to sustain the experience of directionlessness, whereby we are still in the here and now and consequently are able to respond fully and with immediacy to the moment — aware of, yet not inappropriately distracted by, the stimuli around and within us — ready to move on to the next gestalt. We can make a differentiation between the fertile void, where that experience becomes the fertile ground of growth, and the futile void, where the experience is felt as empty, meaningless or frightening and the person either lapses into despair or hurries to fill the gap with some sort of mental or physical activity. The person in our example lies relaxed and at peace with herself until the sensation of wanting to get out of bed emerges.

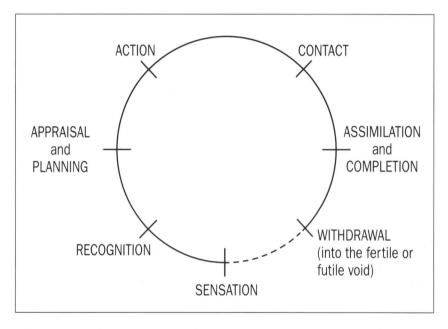

Figure 4   *The cycle of experience*

We realize that a detailed account of these stages may give the impression that the cycle is a somewhat ponderous and time-consuming experience. This is certainly not necessarily the case. For instance, while writing about the cycle, one of us felt a sensation on her skin. Glancing down she saw (and recognized immediately!) that it was a wasp. Instantly, she felt a pang of fear and raised her hand to flick it off. The feeling of finger against insect, the sight of the departing wasp and the beginnings of relief and satisfaction were almost simultaneous. It took a few further moments for her fear to subside and for her to feel relaxed before the gestalt was completed. This whole cycle occurred so quickly that she could return to the task of writing with scarcely a break.

At other times, the cycle may take much longer. It can be used to describe, for example, a pianist learning a new piece of music: from the initial desire, through the learning and practising to the full contact of the performance of the finished piece, followed by the satisfaction and the eventual withdrawal of interest in that piece. This may take minutes, days or months, depending upon the standard of the pianist. The cycle of experience can also be used as a way of understanding the stages of a bereavement process or of the counselling journey as the client first becomes aware of her feelings and thoughts, then gradually begins to take charge of her life.

Disturbances in the Cycle

It is inevitable that many potential cycles are not completed. It would be impossible for us to bring every stimulus into full awareness and respond to it. There are thousands of stimuli that, by necessity, we must ignore moment by moment in order to get on with our lives. Right now, as we write this book, our senses are being assailed by a myriad of stimuli. On the inside, these may be the many and various physiological changes that our bodies go through constantly, or the memories, thoughts and feelings of all the other things in our lives which are unconnected with writing a book. In the external world, we have before us a view of the countryside and we could stop and focus on the colours and shapes, the sounds and smells. The list would be endless, but we choose for the most part to ignore these stimuli in favour of our immediate and chosen task of engagement with writing. We bridge or make a premature ending to the potential gestalt by saying, "The writing is more important at this point in time." In this instance, we are making a choice in focusing on our current work.

However, there are also times when we may interrupt the flow of a gestalt cycle without awareness, in a way that limits our full experience of meeting our current need in the here and now. Difficulties can occur in our lives when there is a disturbance at any stage in the cycle which leads to an inappropriate incompletion or to the 'skewing' of the subsequent stages. A counsellor will help the client to become aware of disturbances they may have at various points, so that they can explore how and sometimes even why they have that disturbance. It may be that at some time they disturbed the natural flow of their cycle in a way and at a time when it was important for them to do so. It may have seemed vital not to upset their parents; it may be that the particular adjustment solved a problem at the time. Perhaps they even thought their life was in danger. In Gestalt, this disturbance of the natural flow of experience is called a 'creative adjustment' to honour the fact that the child who first developed it was doing something creative in response to a perceived problem or danger. It was something that worked at the time. The 'creative adjustment' then became a habit which may not be useful in the present day. The resolving of disturbances in the cycle of experience is an important feature of Gestalt counselling and we will be returning to it later.

For the moment we will mention some of the ways disturbances at particular stages may be seen in our clients — and ourselves. This is certainly not a comprehensive list, but some ideas to provoke thought and investigation. You will notice that different disturbances may, for different reasons, sometimes cause the same problem.

A disturbance around the sensation stage may manifest itself in different ways. Commonly, a person who is disturbed at this stage may have difficulty identifying and differentiating bodily sensations which can lead to poor self-care, or an inability to know what they want in certain circumstances. They may seem unaware of their surroundings. They may suffer from chronic ailments as their body somatizes stress. They may seem withdrawn and flat, report feeling little or no emotion, and have few friends. Occasionally, with extreme disturbance, they may practise self-harming behaviour.

It is important to mention another disturbance that can happen at the sensation stage of the cycle. This is oversensitization.

Occasionally, individuals have difficulty in screening out the many stimuli that bombard their senses. They are constantly responding to the world around them and within them and they have difficulty in selecting the stimuli which are relevant to them at any particular moment. Frequently, they have trouble in clearly recognizing and thinking about what their sensations are and what they might mean. A client may seem agitated and jumpy. He may be unable to focus on what is foreground for him. Everything seems foreground. In this case a counsellor would not concentrate on helping a client to heighten his sensation and awareness. Instead she would teach the client to slow down, reduce his energy levels and find ways of managing his sensations.

A disturbance at the recognition stage can lead to a person having difficulty in naming their sensations and therefore in identifying their needs. They may come to counselling knowing that 'there is something wrong' but unable to say what it is. Alternatively, a person for whom there is a disturbance at this stage may appear very impulsive and highly energized. Here, the person is aware of feeling sensations, does not properly name them or 'appraise' them and goes straight to action in a way that is clearly unthought-out.

Disturbances at the appraisal and planning stage may lead to depression or anxiety as the person mobilizes their energy but fails satisfactorily to channel it into effective action. Indecision and worrying may also be a feature. Also, this stage builds on the meaning making which started at recognition. It is an important stage for making sense of our experience. If a client seems to be making sense of a situation in a way that does not seem logical or likely, it may well be that there is a disturbance here.

A disturbance at the appraisal to action stage can show in procrastination. At the action to contact stage, on the contrary, a disturbance may be seen in a person who is excessively busy and active. They may complain of stress or they may not. Either way, they seem to go on and on repeating an experience and not feeling as if they are 'making it'. They are sometimes identified as 'workaholic'. They may be perfectionists trying to 'get it right' but not succeeding in giving themselves fully to the contact with a task or a person. They may have many friends but few intimates. The 'Casanova syndrome' is seen in men who interrupt their experience at this stage. They go from sexual conquest to sexual conquest, but they avoid the real contact of intimacy.

People who have difficulty in being satisfied may have problems at the assimilation and completion stage. They seem always to be disappointed that they have not been perfect in whatever they undertake. If a client complains of not being good enough, it is interesting to notice whether this indicates a disturbance at appraisal, where their plans are anxiously abandoned as not being 'right', or at contact, where they deprive themselves of the full experience, or at the assimilation and completion stage, where, although contact has been made, dissatisfaction sets in. Again, a sort of 'workaholic' style can be seen here.

Disturbance around the assimilation/completion and withdrawal stages may be suspected in clients where there are issues to do with ending. This difficulty with ending can be manifested in many ways, not just in relation to unresolved bereavements, obvious losses or separations. The individual may have a great fear of being alone. They may have immense trouble choosing amongst different things because of the loss of the 'unchosen' items. They may have difficulty in finishing generally — from leaving at the end of sessions, to finishing their sentences. A client who keeps talking until you are forced to interrupt him may well have some disturbance at this stage in the cycle.

We have given some general indicators about the way disturbances in the cycle of experience can show themselves. In Gestalt, we often use the term 'interruptions' to describe the active, here-and-now process by which the person disturbs the cycle's natural flow. The word 'interruption' is used to indicate that the original cycle is literally interrupted in some way. However, it is important to remember that the interruption is not necessarily a simple breaking off. It can take the form of a distortion, a moderation, a displacement, a replacement, and so on.

Interruptions to the Cycle of Experience

There are seven ways of interrupting the cycle: (1) desensitization, (2) deflection, (3) introjection, (4) projection, (5) retroflection, (6) egotism and (7) confluence. These seven processes, or interruptions, may occur at any point in the cycle. In other words, we may interrupt our experience in any of the above seven ways during sensation, recognition, appraisal and mobilization, action, contact, assimilation/completion and withdrawal. Frequently, a number of these processes may combine to make a break in the natural cycle and create an alternative closure. This could be healthy or unhealthy for the person: it is healthy and appropriate when I hold back my urge to kick the man who pushes ahead of me in the queue; it may be inappropriate if I hold back from sharing my feelings of sadness with a trusted friend. Before going on to describe the interruptions in detail, we want to add that they are 'not absolutes, but metaphors' (Ian Greenway, friend and colleague, 1994, personal communication). They are used to help in understanding something which is unique to every individual, and should not be used as labels.

Desensitization

Desensitization is the process by which a person numbs their natural ability to sense their world. This means they dull their ability to see, hear, feel, taste, smell or touch, or any combination of these. Clearly, desensitization is most often observed at the sensitization phase of the cycle of experience, where it also has the most deleterious effect. The person shuts down their sensations so they literally have no response to the many internal and external stimuli of their world. For example, as Arthur enters the consulting room, he bangs his elbow sharply on the door jamb but seems oblivious to this both then and when asked about it later in the session. Neither is he aware of any discomfort in his body as he sits awkwardly on the edge of his chair. This helps inform the counsellor that Arthur will need to focus on becoming more aware of his bodily sensations and contact functions. Desensitization, at this point in the cycle, can range from someone who is not in touch with their own body to a full catatonic state.

Another aspect of sensitization, apart from desensitization, is that of oversensitization. Here, as opposed to being numbed, the organism is overstimulated with sensation. This oversensitization can lead to the avoidance and neglect of contact with the more appropriate stimulus which, even if painful, may need to be observed and resolved. Desensitization and oversensitization can be achieved with the use of certain substances such as nicotine, alcohol, drugs, caffeine, carbohydrates, sugar and so on.

Desensitization can, of course, take place at any other phase of the cycle. For example, Molly has worked hard and with enthusiasm for her music exam. When she eventually goes to the award ceremony, she desensitizes her full experience of satisfaction with her success; she does not hear when her name is called out to announce her distinction.

Sometimes, however, rather than impede the organism, desensitization actually facilitates it. In the final game of an important tennis match, one of the players may choose to ignore a sharp pain in her knee in order to win the match. This raises the observable fact that in terms of self-regulation the tennis player's desensitization interrupts the natural cycle of her care of her limbs. However, in the parallel cycle of achieving a long-worked-for prize this desensitization occurs at the contact phase. What differentiates a healthy from an unhealthy interruption is usually the element of awareness and choice involved. By and large, negative interruptions occur 'compulsively'.

You the reader might begin to familiarize yourself with this concept of desensitization by identifying how it manifests in your own life, both generally and at this moment. Take your attention away from this book and notice places in your body which you may be holding in an uncomfortable way. For instance, you may be crossing your legs in such a way that the back of one knee is numb. You may be ignoring a biological need, such as hunger. Sometimes, if the mind is being nourished, the bodily needs become background. In order to reconnect with the natural sensitivity of your body, we suggest that you experiment with different positions until you find one in which you are accounting for all of your body. Many people in 'modern' civilization require the help of spectacles. Sometimes this is brought about by the overuse of close sight for reading, writing, using computers and so on. In societies where people do not do so much of this close type of work, eyesight is often better. We suggest that you devise a programme of time structuring which ensures that you have at least five minutes per hour of reading which involves looking at something in the environment nearer the horizon.

In general, are there things in your life that you allow to become extreme before you take notice of them? Do you suddenly realize that you are very hungry or exhausted? Do you often find that you have eaten too much? Do you find bruises on yourself and not know how you got them? Begin to identify the areas in which you desensitize. This is the first step towards resensitization.

Alternatively you may be oversensitized, as described earlier. Do you find yourself overwhelmed and overstimulated by the world around you? Do you have difficulty in selecting relevant data? You may wish to practise slowing down, withdrawing into yourself and deciding what you want before facing the world.

Deflection

Deflection is the process whereby we divert energy from its natural path to an alternative one. It is a way of causing some stimulus from the environment to ricochet away from making an impact upon us. This interruption may occur at any point on the cycle of experience. It is often used at the recognition phase in order to defend against some discomforting sensation. For example, Hilda looks sad when talking of her struggle to make a good relationship with her husband and, when one of her group members says how sad the situation sounds, Hilda says, "Well, we have been married for 18 years." When encouraged to say how she feels, Hilda then deflects by asking, "Well, what do you mean by 'sad'?" At the action phase of the cycle of experience, deflection can be seen when Tim, who is about to tell another group member how angry he is about her repeated absences, comments on the pattern of her jersey instead.

Deflection can be very useful at times when full recognition of the situation might make it more difficult to complete. Jean is terrified of dental work and chooses to deflect from her terror by trying to remember all the verses of a song so that the dentist may complete her filling as efficiently as possible.

You the reader can, if you wish, start to explore your own deflections. What are the things you do not want to think about? If you genuinely tried to answer that question, you will probably have found that you quickly distracted yourself by thinking of or doing something else. Do you know what it is that you were avoiding, what unpleasant feelings or thoughts seemed unbearable to you? As you slowly read the following list, notice which items you flinch away from: bread, books, spiders, trees, death, Mozart, cancer, sex, Hitler, lollipop sticks, dentists, Barry Manilow, caves, clouds, birds, ice, polystyrene, starvation.

Introjection

Introjection is the process of absorbing or swallowing whole some rule, message, model and so on that is presented to the organism from outside itself. This is the most pervasive of all interruptions to healthy functioning. An introject is that which has in the past been accepted without discrimination and reverberates in the present. It is possible to introject at any time of life as we learn and model ourselves on people in our environment. However, most introjection is done in the early years of childhood when we are most vulnerable and impressionable, dependent for our survival upon those powerful and loved adults whose approval we desperately need. It is from our parents therefore (or primary caretakers) that we receive and swallow most of the axioms we will continue to use in order to make meaning of life, relationships and ourselves. There are countless ways in which we introject from the world around us: the food we eat, the way we dress, the types of relationship we seek, what we deem to be well-mannered or otherwise, and so on. Advertisers depend on the phenomenon of introjection to have their products bought without careful consideration of the act.

We may notice introjection at the appraisal and mobilization phase of the gestalt cycle. Andrew seems on the verge of tears but suddenly says, "It's too silly a thing to cry about." Later in the counselling session he remembers that his mother often told the boys in his family not to make a fuss about silly, little things.

Celia is exploring the idea of changing her career by listing jobs that she might do. Her counselling group soon confront her with the realization that her list includes only stereotypically female options such as nurse, secretary and nursery school teacher. One of the group members says, "You are brilliant at figures; why not include accountancy and so on?" Immediately, Celia becomes uncomfortable and anxious. After further exploration of her experience she realizes that in her family of origin the men were traditionally the 'clever' ones and the females were caring and homely. A female accountant would have been seen as too unfeminine. As she begins to recall the pervasiveness of her introject, she remembers how her mother had written in her autograph book, "Be good sweet maid, and let who can be clever..."

Introjection also occurs at other points in the cycle and usually underpins another interruption. For instance, Hilda, who deflected from her sadness, had the injunction, "Don't get upset", while Molly, who desensitized her pleasure at her success, believed that she "shouldn't get overexcited".

Naturally, it would be a great mistake to start to reject all that we have learned from our parents and family. Introjecting rules for living is part of the way in which we learn and keep ourselves safe. A beginning stage in the learning process is to copy, that is introject, the modeller. Later on, as our skills develop, we begin to hone our style better to suit our individual needs and talents. A child learns "Don't run into the road", "Be polite to people", "Eat healthily", "This is how to read", and so on, which are often pieces of learning vital for living in society. There are many introjects which, even when we become aware that they were our parents' opinion rather than THE TRUTH, we choose to retain because we find them useful and appropriate: for instance, "It is important to be respectful to people", "Violence is wrong", "Beauty is to be treasured".

Another important factor in considering introjects is culture. Many of the introjects we all hold were given to us by the culture in which we live. They come via our parents, schools, friends, neighbours, ministers and many other sources. There will be differences in beliefs and values between people from different countries, and also between different groups in apparently the same society: Irish, Asian, West Indian, northern working class, white middle class, Roman Catholic, Methodist, and so on. It is important when working with clients to be aware, as far as possible, of our own cultural introjects as well as those of our clients. In that way we can try to avoid inadvertently imposing our frame of reference on the counselling setting. We can also treat with respect the culture of our client, inviting him to be aware of the influence that his culture has had on him and allowing him to work within that frame of reference if he chooses.

We suggest you now take a moment to think about what you

believe concerning asking for help. Do you, for example, say things like, "Oh, I don't want to burden others with my problems" or "If you want something done well you must do it yourself" or "Ask and you shall be given" or "I want — won't get!" or other responses? Almost certainly, some of your replies will be direct introjects of parental messages and modelling.

Experiment with almost any area of your life and see how influenced you have been in your apparent personal choices. Are these beliefs about 'the way to be' still relevant or might you want to change them? If you wish to improve your discrimination and combat introjection, it can be helpful to use certain basic questions regularly — "Do I want this?", "Do I agree with this?", "Does this suit me?" — and some basic self-instructions: "Chew a while before swallowing", "I can have my own fresh opinion about this."

Projection

Projection is the process of disowning some aspect of self and placing it in something outside — whether a person, animal or object. A person projects when they imagine that they know what another person is feeling or thinking or why they are doing something. Sometimes our projections are appropriately based on life experience. For instance, when Robert is scowling and answering in monosyllables, I project that he may be angry with me and I decide that this is not the moment to give him a hug. I do this without asking him and my conclusion is based on the fact that usually, when people behave like this, they are angry. I choose to interrupt the gestalt that I was forming. Equally, when a colleague approaches me smiling, with outstretched hand, I imagine that she is being friendly on the basis of my past experiences of people who have behaved in this way.

Artists use a form of projection when they turn their ideas into an image on canvas, in clay, and so on. Architects use projection when planning a shopping centre in order to imagine what facilities will be needed. Or we use projection when we are packing our suitcase to go on holiday. We would be lost without projection — as, indeed, is true of all the interruptions.

Projection becomes an interruption to the natural cycle of experience when I do not meet another person as they are in the here and now, because I am fantasizing something about their attitude and do not check to see if my fantasy is true. I am barely aware that it is my fantasy. It feels as if it is something I 'know'.

Frequently, projections have extra dimensions. We have already talked about the powerful influence that our parents have on us when we are children. Our introjects include images of our parents and other significant figures as they responded to us, and we carry the expectation that others will respond to us in the same way. Therefore, when Andrew held back his tears, he not only activated the introject about not making a fuss, he also projected his mother's face on the counsellor and thought, "She'll think I'm silly." Susan, whose father was stern and distant, projected her father onto any significant man and imagined that he would not be interested in her. In the group, she did not make contact with any of the men because she assumed they would not want her to. In that way, she interrupted her natural desire to reach out and get close to others.

Often, people project as a result of an injunction which forbids them to be a certain way. A woman may believe that she is bad if she feels angry. Therefore, when she does begin to feel angry, she has to cut off that part of herself. A man may feel deeply ashamed of his physical weakness and try to disown that. Using projection, a person might take that split-off part of themselves and see it in someone else, where it is more easily accepted — or even where they can criticize it with a feeling of superiority. Thus Deirdre, who must not feel anger, imagines that her counsellor is angry and feels frightened. John, who was bad at sports, despises Alan for being small and weak.

Besides our more negative qualities we also project positive attributes that we have not yet integrated. Jess, who had very low self-esteem, projected her intelligence and vivacity onto Judith (who, incidentally, reminded her of her younger sister — the favourite in the family) and felt both stupid and resentful. She was astounded when group members said, "But that's exactly what we see in you."

When projection occurs at the action stage, having mobilized their energy, a person changes their direction as a result of their fantasies and fixed gestalts. This particularly happens in the process of making contact with another person: at recognition they misinterpret the signals that the other is giving them; at appraisal they limit their options which are based on their projection; at contact they lose their true awareness of self and other as they relate to the person they imagine to be there.

A form of projection, in actuality a mixture of projection and retroflection, is named 'proflection'. Proflection is the process whereby we do for others what we hope they will do for us. Normally, people who proflect have an injunction which forbids them to have needs or ask for what they want. Out of their awareness, they have a need and they translate that into action towards another. A person is proflecting, therefore, who offers you tea when they are thirsty, strokes your back when they want attention, talks lovingly to the dog when they need to hear such kindnesses, and so forth.

In order to recognize some attribute of your own that you are projecting while you read this book, let yourself know some opinion you have had about the authors. Is this a valid opinion based on the contents and style of what you have read or are some of those opinions disowned qualities which belong to you?

One of the immediate ways of beginning to 'reown' what has been projected could be to allow yourself to consider some of these questions: "In what ways am I like this too?", "What part of myself am I choosing to ignore when I take an extreme stand?" When did you last ask a friend or family member if they would like something, when in fact you really wanted that very thing? Becoming honest about your own needs and desires will prevent the use of proflection.

Retroflection

Retroflection is a process whereby energy which would naturally be directed outwards is turned inwards: a person who experiences the impulse to action in speech, gesture or deed blocks the flow of their energy and turns it back into themselves. Have you ever been at a concert and needed to sneeze during a quiet part of the music? If you did a sort of silent inward explosion that created movement in your body but no noise, that is retroflection. When you stop yourself yawning in the middle of a conversation, when you restrain yourself from pushing to the front of a queue, when you hold back from snapping at the traffic warden, you are retroflecting. It is easy to see how, without retroflection, society could not function harmoniously.

There are two types of retroflection. In the first, a person uses their energy on themselves instead of allowing their healthy urge to use that energy on or with another. Here I do to myself what I would naturally want to do to you. One of the most common retroflections that counsellors meet is probably retroflected anger. Instead of being able to be appropriately angry with someone, a person swallows back and contains their ire. This person may have an introject about expressing anger. It may be that anger is bad generally, or it may be that "Other people won't like you" or "You mustn't hurt their feelings" or "Don't make a fuss". Whatever the reason, the person retroflects their anger and may turn it on themselves, criticizing themselves for being stupid or blaming themselves for whatever happened. Such patterns are often established in childhood when the young person turns their anger on themselves, both out of fear of the parents' reprisals and also often out of a need to 'keep the parents good'. For a little child it is often quite frightening to believe that their parents may not always be perfect.

There are many other examples of this type of retroflection. Susan, who believed that the men in the group would not be interested in her, retroflected her want to show affection to Robert. Instead of stroking him, she began to stroke her own arm. Joe nearly shouted with surprise, then bit his lip as he remembered 'not to make a fool' of himself. When Des was feeling needy he did not ask for the support he wanted. He held it in and began to agitate by jiggling his foot as his tension mounted.

In this way the retroflector is both the activator and the receiver. She puts herself in the place of the environment and relates to herself. For that reason, retroflection is most often seen at the action and contact stages of the cycle. The person holds back action, turns it on herself, and then dwells exclusively on her own feelings and thoughts instead of making contact with the world around her.

The Gestalt philosophy which views a person as a whole, believing that the body, mind and emotions cannot be separated, can lead us to some interesting hypotheses about health. With this holistic approach we may speculate that much physical disease has emotional and mental contributory factors as well as physical ones. Retroflected emotions, the calling back into the system of energy which is fundamentally required by the organism to push outwards, contribute to our physical malfunctioning. Like pressure-cookers, we humans need to let off the steam of our feelings and emotions. If this is not possible through normal channels, alternatives are found. These different ways of expelling energy often result in a distortion of the organism. We could hypothesize: retroflected *sorrow* can be manifested through illnesses such as colds which cause our eyes and nose to stream; retroflected *angry* energy may find release through the more 'acid' illnesses, such as ulceration; retroflected *fear* could be seen in getting feverish; and so on.

The second form of retroflection occurs when a person does to or for themselves the things that they wish the environment would do to or for them. Here I do to myself what I would naturally want you to do to or for me. The man who wants to be nurtured, but cannot ask, lights a cigarette. The woman whose parents did not set appropriate limits, longs for the environment to give her clear feedback, to set boundaries for her. She sets boundaries for herself by criticizing herself in a manner far more harsh than anyone else could do, and setting herself impossible tasks.

There are times when it is appropriate to learn to retroflect. Brenda had a history of losing jobs for having 'a poor attitude'. In the counselling group, she explained how yet again she had lost her temper with her new boss when he asked her to repeat a piece of work. Brenda had had an overbearing and bullying father and had a tendency to become very defensive and then to attack if she felt criticized by a man. The group helped her to understand that her angry feelings did not represent the facts and that a person who wants to keep their job sometimes must restrain their impulse towards an angry outburst, even in the face of real or suspected criticism.

Becoming aware how you treat yourself may well be the first step in identifying ways in which you choose to retroflect your energy rather than to propel it outwards. Do you chew your cuticles or bite your nails? Do you bite or suck your lips? Do you have regular gestures which involve some form of self-stroking?

There may be some simple actions you can take to undo your more minor retroflections. Instead of biting back your anger and clenching your fingers into your palms you could spring open your hands as though to free some trapped insect from inside them. You could tear up a paper handkerchief. One person, who knew it would be unwise to voice her anger in a meeting, went immediately for a walk in a wood where she could safely release her angry shouts. Many retroflections, because they were developed as the best protection available at some past time, require patient and careful undoing and often require and deserve outside help.

Egotism

Egotism is the process of self-monitoring or 'spectatoring'. This prevents true involvement in any experience. Egotism can be useful for, say, the beginner learning to drive, or the counsellor who listens to an audiotape of himself in order to self-supervise and improve his work. It can also be vital to those who need to increase awareness of self — as with many of the awareness exercises described earlier. However, it can be an incapacitating interruption of contact with the internal and external environment.

Egotism can occur at any stage of the gestalt cycle. However, this process may especially interrupt the flow of energy at the assimilation and completion stage. Instead of being aware of the sense of completeness and satisfaction that would then naturally occur, the person stands outside himself and is aware of looking at himself to assess how he is performing or has performed. Such individuals do not refer to an inner feeling to decide the degree to which their gestalt has been completed. They become external observers who scrutinize them. For example, Sandy, after weeping copiously about the loss of a friend, finishes and sits back. Rather than be with herself and her counsellor, who has shared the experience, she immediately starts to comment on and assess her work: whether it was enough; how loudly she had cried; what a good client she had been; she had noticed that her hands had been quite childlike; she thought there was a connection to her mother; and so on.

Egotism may interfere with real contact because the person steps back from contact and, instead, watches themselves making contact. Egotism can take the form of pride and admiration of the self or of criticism and denigration. In the latter case, the person is painfully aware of how she must be appearing to others and imagines at every step what critical thoughts they are having. Frequently, they believe that, "If people really knew me, they would think I'm worthless" and feel a need to hide.

It is important as counsellors to be aware that our tendency towards egotism can be increased by any theory which encourages self-analysis. Gestaltists' focus on self-awareness can lead, through egotism, to a form of self-absorbed introspection which interrupts the natural flow of the cycle of experience and loses the real, unpremeditated and unreserved contact with the environment which is the hallmark of true awareness. Laura Perls (1992) says that 'embarrassment is the inevitable awareness of lack of support that accompanies the initial exciting contact with any new experience'. She is pointing out that, if we meet an experience freshly and openly, without controlling it in any way, we will feel unbalanced, unsettled, vulnerable. We should not avoid that experience through egotism, or any other interruption to contact, but be willing to meet it fully.

In order to experience egotism you could try giving a running commentary to yourself in a given situation. For example, as you talk to a friend, you could describe to yourself everything you are doing and saying. "I am smiling kindly and taking an interest in my friend. Now I am looking quizzical and my friend must be wondering what I'm thinking. I'm asking him to tell me more about his situation. I am listening with my head on one side." Can you feel the way in which egotism prevents real contact with your friend?

Confluence

Confluence is the process of merging with the environment so that the awareness of separateness is lost. The negative aspect of this process is that confluence prevents differentiation and individualization. The confluent person does not differentiate between their experience and another's. They are not in touch with their or the other's individuality. For example, Felicity and Tom have been married for nine years and have both developed the habit of using the pronoun 'we' when really talking about their individual proclivities. The counsellor and client need to be aware (and beware) that the sort of closeness, the empathic meeting and the unique quality of the relationship offered in the counselling setting may have the effect of inviting and encouraging confluence.

In the confluent relationship, the individual, once merged, has difficulty in separating or letting go of an experience. This causes particular difficulties at the withdrawal stage of the cycle of experience, when we must be willing, having completed a gestalt, to let go of it and withdraw into the 'fertile void', ready to respond to the next emerging figure. At the end of sessions, a confluent client may find it very difficult to leave, producing last-minute things to say and do as they struggle not to let go of the experience.

Confluence can also occur at any other stage of the cycle and can result in a reluctance to let go of an idea, a feeling or a situation. For instance, Lucy, trying to generate options to solve a work problem, became confluent with one idea and seemed unable to relinquish it.

Confluence is particularly relevant in relation to couples. A confluent couple cannot explore or experience their full individuality. Confluence precludes creative conflict within the relationship. The need to maintain homeostasis is such that there is no room for anything new, unexpected or experimental. Despite their desire for confluence, the partners often end up feeling bored.

However, as with all the interruptions, confluence has its positive aspects. We need moments of confluence in order to be empathic with one another. Hence the well known Native American Indian saying that exhorts us not to judge a man before 'walking a mile in his moccasins'. Intense intimate contact also involves moments of confluence. There is appropriate confluence between a mother and baby. Frequently, people talk of 'losing' themselves in the experience of sex. Such positive confluence, however, is followed by appropriate withdrawal.

Bob Resnick (1985) has made some important theoretical contributions with reference to couples. He identifies a confluence —isolation continuum, in which people move from isolation, to separation, to contact, to intimacy, to confluence and then to withdrawal. Figure 5 illustrates the continuum. This model shows how in healthy relating we need to have the capacity for both distance and closeness and to move between the two. It is important for us to be able to be in any of the positions.

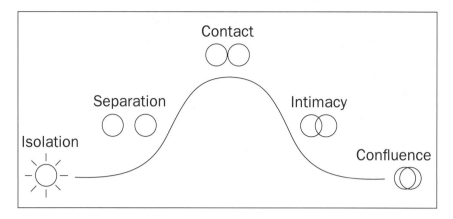

Figure 5   *The confluence—isolation continuum*

At this moment you, the reader, could identify some examples of the way you let yourself become confluent. Let yourself think of some very close relationship you have. This may be a partner, parent, child, sibling or friend. Make a list of things you both like, starting each one with 'we'. Check with the other person its accuracy for them. In order to prevent confluence you could think of another person with whom you are close and find things that you both like and dislike and things that one likes which the other does not.

Unfinished Business

Perls (1976) called interruptions to the cycle 'unfinished business'. He recognized that, until we have completed such business (closed the gestalt, made whole), we cannot be fully in the here and now. Our awareness of the present will be influenced by the incompleteness of our past experiences. We need to complete our experience before we can withdraw our energy from it. Of course, there will be many situations in our lives which we cannot complete at the time. We must delay the fulfilment of our needs until later and we must learn to cope with that delay. This is easier to do with some experiences than with others. You may find it easy to postpone the essay you have to write in order to chat to a friend. However, while talking, if you are waiting for news about your sister's operation you will find it difficult to give your full attention to your friend until the phone call has come through. Clearly, the level of pleasure and satisfaction attached to the need plays a part. You may happily delay visiting your dentist for weeks, but if a tooth starts aching, your need to make that visit will nag for your urgent attention until it is satisfied.

Delaying the completion of a task, curbing the full expression of a feeling or halting the development of an idea all take energy. We may be able to bracket one thing off in order to deal with another, but the very act of setting and keeping it aside involves a lot of energy. Richard tells his counsellor about his stress and exhaustion at work, and that he has been criticized for poor performance. He works as a secretary in a busy firm and talks with some distress about a typical day. He is typing an important letter. He is halfway through when the telephone rings. It is someone placing a long order. He begins to jot down the list. The internal phone rings. He excuses himself to the first caller to take the call from his boss, who asks him to find a file for her. Meanwhile, a colleague has appeared to ask what kind of sandwich he would like for lunch. In the space of a few minutes his attention is drawn to several tasks, some of which, by necessity, remain incomplete. In order to begin to deal with these tasks, he needs to prioritize, to withdraw his attention temporarily from some while giving his attention to others. By lunch-time, the original letter he was typing is still incomplete and he has not delivered the customer's order to the relevant department. It is no surprise that he is exhausted — not just from doing the work he has done but in using his energy to withdraw his attention temporarily from the uncompleted tasks. If he had been able to ignore the demands completely or to choose not to respond to them, that would have been different. But he could not. Even over his sandwich he finds it hard not to think about finishing off the letter. In talking this over, Richard begins to realize how he is stressing himself and starts discussing ways in which he could make his life easier for himself, by cutting down on some of the demands in his life and making sure to complete some of his tasks come what may.

Putting aside incomplete gestalts for our later attention is obviously something we do constantly in our everyday lives. It is our natural way of coping with and dealing with the many demands of living. However, there are some experiences which, for various reasons, we may bracket off and not return our attention to until much later, if at all. When we were describing the need for completion we talked about Jim and his feelings of hurt and anger at being left by Stephanie. He set aside his feelings at the time and returned to them only when meeting Stephanie again at a later stage. However, during this time of 'soldiering on', he used up a great deal of energy in not allowing himself to be aware fully of what he felt, hence his recurring 'depression'. If he could have been more attuned to himself, he could have closed the incomplete gestalt even in Stephanie's absence by sharing and expressing his feelings with a friend or counsellor.

A similar example of the way the unfinished business presses to be completed is contained in the psychoanalytic principle of the repetition compulsion. Arthur's mother died when he was three. Ever since then, both in his childhood and also as an adult, Arthur has seemed to be searching for someone to take care of him. The women he falls for tend to be motherly types, frequently older than him, and often have an old-fashioned look to them.

There is another way in which incomplete gestalts can affect us, sometimes to our detriment. In a counselling session, Jill says she does not know what to talk about. There are so many issues that worry her — her relationships, her course work, a fight with her mother, and so on. But she says that she does not know which one to choose to talk about. The counsellor asks her what seems most important — most 'foreground' — at the moment. Jill stares out of the window for a while and then says, "I don't know. I don't know what is important. I don't know what I'm feeling. [*She laughs nervously*] I don't think I know who I am."

The counsellor suggests that she experiment with knowing who she is now: "What are you feeling now — in your body?"

JILL: Well, I feel OK. My leg is a little stiff [*moves her leg to ease it*] and I'm aware I need to pee.

COUNSELLOR: Do you want to do something about that need?

JILL: I don't know. I don't want to waste the time, there's so many important things to look at — but OK, I will.

[Jill gets up and goes off to the bathroom. She returns smiling.]

JILL: I understand now. I spend so much time thinking and worrying about all sorts of things that I get out of touch with me. I need to pay attention to my 'here and now' needs and wants, and act on those more — then I'll know who I am.

Fixed Gestalts

●

Many incomplete gestalts originate in childhood and, if we do not recognize them and pay attention to ways in which we can complete them, they will affect us throughout our adult lives. Perls used the term 'premature closure' to describe the interruption of an experience in a way that shuts down the natural response and often replaces it with some other behaviour. This may happen in traumatic circumstances but more often happens as a result of the repetition of restrictions and injunctions from an environment which disapproves of some behaviours and encourages others. A typical example is that of Peter, who learned to interrupt his tears when he was sad, as his parents repeatedly said, "Big boys don't cry." They also approvingly said, "That's my brave boy," when he was assertive or angry. In compliance, Peter learnt to retroflect his sadness and turn it into anger. This is likely to happen again and again in the family, so the pattern of getting angry instead of sad becomes what is called a 'fixed gestalt'.

Florence was sent to her room as a child if she became upset. She was told she could come downstairs again when "you're nice Florence again". Alone in her room, unable to manage the distress she felt, she retroflected her feelings and deflected her energy into tidying her books and toys. As an adult, Florence used the same deflection of tidying the home when she was upset. In counselling, she realized that she was trying to 'tidy away' the parts of herself of which her parents had disapproved. The introjection of 'be a nice Florence' she interpreted to mean that strong feelings were somehow messy and should be cleaned up.

Much of the work done in Gestalt counselling focuses on identifying and undoing fixed gestalts and completing these incomplete gestalts from the past so that they no longer impinge upon the client in the present. When Caroline was a child, her need of care and comfort was mostly ignored by her parents. Sometimes she would cry for their attention, sometimes she would get angry, but when all her attempts to get care and comfort were ignored, she too learnt to ignore those needs. She did, however, still have the drive to complete. Therefore she 'completed' the gestalt of these needs by telling herself she was 'too needy' and 'selfish' and must learn to put others before herself. Saying these things provided some sort of closure as she found a reason to close down her feelings. This response became a pattern which continued into her adult life. Indeed, as an adult, despite her loneliness and continuous feeling of emptiness, she had postponed coming to counselling for many years. She saw counselling as 'self-indulgent' and many times in the initial counselling sessions would attempt to ignore her own needs by looking after the counsellor: "How are you? You look tired" or "Oh, you don't want to hear all about this. You must be really bored." Over time, however, within the trust and consistency of the counselling relationship, she began to express her needs and more adequately complete her need for care and comfort within and outside the counselling sessions.

Exercises

●

1 Wholeness

(a) For a few moments, look up from this book and notice your surroundings. Without paying attention to any one thing in particular, allow your eyes to take in all that you can see and create a whole out of your visual experience.

(b) As you are seeing 'the whole', be aware of your other senses. What are you hearing? What can you smell? What can you taste? What are you sensing physically and emotionally? As simultaneously as possible, be aware of your whole experience.

(c) Now choose one thing within your environment and focus upon this thing, allowing it to become figure while all else becomes ground. Notice how it is still part of a greater whole. Notice how its edges are defined by the ground. Notice how its colour is relevant to the rest of the environment.

(d) Move your attention to something else. What has happened to your experience of the first thing on which you focused? How has your perception of it changed?

(e) Now move yourself to a different part of the room. How does the change of your position within the whole situation alter that whole? What is your experience now of the things on which you focused before?

2 Completion

(a) Without looking, make a scribble on a piece of paper. When you look at it, see what image you immediately create out of these random lines. If you do not immediately see the image of something, turn the paper in different directions. Fill in the scribble to better resemble your image. Notice how, in your mind, you add certain parts and delete others in order to make your image complete. This is what you did visually when you first looked.

(b) Place a piece of paper over a page of this book so that it covers about half an inch of the printed words down the left-hand side. Now read a paragraph or so and see how many words, phrases and sentences you can complete despite some words or half-words being hidden.

(c) See if you can read some of these sentences *without* completing them!

Do not lean out of the ....

"Hello," said Joan, "I haven't seen you for ...."

Gestalt counselling emphasizes the here and ....

Too many .... spoil the broth.

I left my .... in San Francisco.

.... well that ends well.

.... off the grass.

(d) Perhaps you are totally up-to-date with all your life's tasks. If not, write down those tasks which you can instantly think of as needing completion over the next few days. Is there one you could do right now? Do it. Now that you have completed it, how do you feel? Do another if you choose.

In this chapter, we have introduced the concept of gestalt formation and described some of its many aspects and their relevance to Gestalt counselling. Gestalt, like most psychological approaches, believes that we are greatly influenced by our past experiences. The experiences we have, the meanings we make of them and the ways in which we respond to them are often patterns of response that may start in early childhood as 'creative adjustments' to our world. However, they become fixed and so much part of us that we become unaware of the fact that we are *choosing* them. The Gestalt approach helps us to develop awareness of who we are, how we are living and how we are relating to the world around us. Through awareness we can begin to stand fully in the reality of the present, seeing things as they are and, in lively and exciting contact, choosing what needs to be chosen. This is a place we knew in our childhood, before we developed our habits of being, and it is a place to which in the depth of our hearts we want to return. We end this chapter with a quote from Laura Perls (1992):

> The aim of Gestalt therapy is the awareness continuum, the freely ongoing gestalt formation where what is of greatest concern and interest to the organism, the relationship, the group or society becomes Gestalt, comes into the foreground where it can be fully experienced and coped with (acknowledged, worked through, sorted out, changed, disposed of, etc.) so that then it can melt into the background (be forgotten or assimilated and integrated) and leave the foreground free for the next relevant gestalt.

Chapter 7

CONNECTEDNESS

Connectedness
●

Nothing exists in isolation. Everything is connected to something else. Everything has a context, a field in which it exists. In order to perceive or understand something, we need to look at the whole situation.

There was a recent television advertisement for a newspaper in which we are first presented with the scene of a smartly dressed businessman walking down the street carrying a brief-case. A skinhead runs up behind him, barges into him and pushes him along the pavement. We seem to be witnessing an attack. But when the scene is repeated, the camera pans back to show a heavy object falling from scaffolding above. The wider context totally alters the meaning of the scene. The younger man is in fact pushing the other out of the way of the falling object and preventing a dreadful accident. This new perspective changes our perception from the extremes of seeing the young man as an attacker to seeing him as a rescuer. The implication of the advertisement is, of course, that this newspaper will be showing events in their widest context and will thereby present us with 'the truth'. The discerning television viewer will bear in mind that there is the even wider context of this being an advertisement and, like all advertisements, it is intended to increase sales. We may appreciate the cleverness of the advertisement but we will need to read the newspaper itself and judge it in comparison with other newspapers before deciding whether we agree with its message.

Here is another example of connectedness and the need to see things in context. While the three of us were engaged in writing, one of Phil's sons came to us and simply said, "Thyme?" All three of us answered him. Phil, knowing his son was cooking an omelette, replied, "On the shelf by the cooker." He had correctly made the connections to his son's communication. Charlotte and Sue, however, not knowing the context of the request but following their natural tendency towards completion and connectedness, heard the request differently. Charlotte answered, "It's ten past one," while Sue replied, "Yes, I think it's time for lunch." Both had heard 'thyme' as 'time' and created their own meaning in their own contexts.

You will see how these examples include wholeness, the formation of a figure completion and also connectedness. These elements are inextricably connected. In fact, we have found it difficult to write about them individually, to write about the parts distinct from the whole, simply because of their interconnectedness.

In looking at people, the Gestalt approach pays attention to the physical, emotional, psychological, social, historical and cultural environment of a person, from which they cannot be disconnected.

Field-Theory

Connectedness is the term we have chosen to describe what is, in effect, field-theory. Kurt Lewin (1935, 1952) saw the individual both within and in relation to the environment. There are several important consequences of this. To understand human beings, we need first to see the whole situation, before attending to the parts. But the environment changes according to circumstances. The individual organizes the totality of the environment according to different situations and different needs, sometimes making one particular aspect figure, sometimes another. Importantly, and with exciting implications for the counselling relationship, humans constellate the field around them so that they in effect create it. In any meeting a field is co-created. The counsellor and client have together a 'betweenness' in which the field is then potentially new every moment.

There are five principles of field-theory (see Malcolm Parlett, 1991).

The Principle of Organization

We derive meaning from perceiving the whole, the total situation. Our example of the advertisement for a newspaper illustrates how meaning is derived differently once we see the whole situation. What in one context takes on one meaning, in another means something different. A stretch of water may be a resource for quenching thirst, a means of travelling from one place to another, a barrier to keep people out, a playground for windsurfers, a washing place, a source of food or a minor detail in the enormity of a landscape. The field is constellated differently according to our need and circumstances.

As Gestalt counsellors, we need to allow the field to develop in order to understand our clients. When Derek begins the session by saying that his father has died, the counsellor does not leap in with condolences but takes time to explore the field of his experience and discover what this means for Derek. His relaxed body posture, the softness of his facial muscles, the evenness of his voice, the fact that he makes good eye contact, the words he uses and what he says with those words, once organized into a whole, may make it clear that right now he is, in fact, much relieved by his father's death.

The Principle of Contemporaneity

Whatever the situation, all that is happening is happening simultaneously *now*. Only from the *present* influence of the field can we make sense of our present experience. Maybe last week you felt angry with someone who ignored you, maybe tomorrow you will feel sad because someone is going away. If you are feeling angry *now*, this can only be because of the present field of your thoughts about that person and the memories of the situation in which you were ignored. Likewise, if you are feeling sad at tomorrow's separation, it can only be that you are currently thinking about the person and imagining their absence. In the former case, the experience has happened and is in the past. In the latter case, the experience has not yet happened. Only your present field of thoughts and fantasies, based in your history of other experiences which also become part of the current field, can explain how you are feeling now.

This does not mean that Gestalt counsellors ignore a client's past or future, but that they will focus attention on the way this past or future is being experienced *now* in the current field which, of course, will include each thought, feeling and action as well as what is happening within the relationship between counsellor and client.

When Derek talks of his relief at the death of his father, the counsellor will be interested in the way that relief is experienced now, how it is currently being expressed (or avoided), how the telling affects the relationship between counsellor and client at this moment, what significance the sudden kicking out of the client's leg may have, how his breathing reflects his current experience, and so on. All that is happening is happening now and is part of Derek's present experience. Even when one thing is made figure, the counsellor pays attention to the simultaneously existing ground.

The Principle of Singularity

Everyone is unique. Each person's experience is unique. As you read this book you will place your own emphasis on certain ideas, make relevance of them, apply them to your experience and make connections with them which are peculiarly your own. Your individual field, of which you are also a part, will influence your experience. Your emotional state, your mental state, your physical state, the context of when, where, why and how you are reading are all part of your unique experience right now.

The focus in Gestalt is upon 'what is'. Any generalizations we make are movements away from this present experiencing, this here-and-now awareness. The Gestalt counsellor does not 'treat' depression, stress, anxiety or phobias but meets and attends to the whole person who, in the present moment, may be experiencing each or any of these generalized descriptions *in their own particular way*.

This does not mean totally ignoring any patterns or consistencies which may have relevance to a person's experience and which may, therefore, be usefully borne in mind. Rather, it places emphasis on perceiving the person's present experience as figure in the current field, not our preconceptions based on generalizations. In our example, the counsellor may be well aware that people in all cultures, in response to the death of a person with whom they have shared some intimacy, over time move through different phases in the process of grieving. However, this experience is unique to each individual. The counsellor will attend to Derek's particular process as he experiences how he is feeling, thinking and behaving *now* in response to his father's death.

The Principle of Changing Process

Nothing is static. Nothing is permanent. Life is always in process. Change is occurring all the time. Though you are still reading this book, the situation has changed and you have moved on to another experience. Even if you read this sentence again immediately, you cannot repeat your original experience of reading it. The field is newly created moment by moment.

The Gestalt approach gives emphasis to constant change, perceiving and describing experience *in process* and avoiding the temptation to use language and definitions which imply permanence. Gestaltists dislike labelling behaviour as pathology. Rather they use the term 'creative adjustment' to describe the development of some behaviour which may seem the best alternative at the time. There is no such thing as a shy person (implying that their behaviour is fixed for all time in all situations in shyness); rather a person is *being shy* right now in this particular situation. Similarly, to label someone as an extrovert is to imply a permanence (and, therefore, a restriction) to their behaviour. Even someone who behaves in an extrovert manner in many situations will not do so all the time in all situations. Rather they are *being extrovert* right now in this particular situation. For all we know, the person described as shy and the person described as extrovert might be one and the same, simply behaving differently according to the circumstances. It is interesting to note that Perls *et al* (1951) define 'the self' as creating itself moment by moment at the contact boundary — the boundary between the person and their environment.

In counselling, the counsellor attends to Derek and his experience as it is right now, aware that his experience is not fixed for all time but is a flowing and ever-changing process. As he talks of his relief at his father's death, the counsellor is aware that this is his experience at the moment. When later he begins to cry, she affirms his current experience. He is neither a 'relieved mourner' nor a 'sad mourner', he is a person in process, moving through the ever-changing field of his perception. When he smiles at some memory of his father he is sharing with the counsellor, he is not necessarily denying his relief or his sadness. Momentarily, he is experiencing feeling warm towards his father as his own singular reality unfolds and moves on.

The Principle of Possible Relevance

Everything in the field has possible meaning. Everything is part of the total organization. According to this principle, we cannot arbitrarily ignore the relevance of anything in the field. As Parlett (1991) writes, 'Gestalt therapists are interested in "the obvious", in rendering afresh what has become invisible and automatic, or is being taken for granted or regarded as of no relevance.' He uses the analogy of looking at a painting and describes how a field theorist will be cognizant not only of the picture but of the style of frame and the context of the exhibition, seeing them all as relevant to their experience of the painting.

Similarly, when working with clients, the Gestalt counsellor does not arbitrarily exclude anything as irrelevant but allows the possible relevance at each moment of, not just the content of what the client is saying, but also, for example, the clothes the person is wearing, their style of speech, their mannerisms, their bodily movements, their breathing, their eye contact, their way of relating to the counsellor. As Derek kicks out his leg while talking about his father's death, the counsellor does not ignore this movement as irrelevant, but may choose to bring Derek's attention to it in order to explore what meaning it may have in the field of his experience. Making figure of what was previously ground, it may transpire that Derek becomes aware of his anger towards his father, of which he has previously been unaware.

In Part III of this book, we will be exploring phenomenology and dialogue in the counselling relationship and we hope to show how these concepts of connectedness translate into practice with our clients. Meanwhile we offer some exercises for your further exploration.

Exercises

●

1 We each make our own connections. We have our own way of constellating and contextualizing. We do not experience things in isolation. For instance, if we imagine an armchair, we may immediately picture a small, cosy room, crammed with furniture and lots of cushions. We may imagine a log-fire, a book, a cup of cocoa which might make us think of a grandparent. Then we may remember sitting on our grandmother's knee listening to a story, feeling safe and warm, and so on. See what connections you make when imagining the following objects or situations:

A jug of milk.

A tractor.

A walking stick.

Two poles with a rope hung between them.

The smell of a bonfire.

The sensation of the wind against your face.

A pile of clothes by a river.

The sound of gunfire.

You might find it interesting to ask your friends to do the same exercise and compare their answers with yours to illustrate how different people's perceptions can be. For instance, in the example of a pile of clothes by a river, did you think of someone doing their laundry, a happy swim in the afternoon sun, or the tragic signs of a suicide? Being aware of how we perceive our world is part of self-awareness. What do you think your associations say about you at this point in time?

2 Think of a friend of yours. What is the immediate context in which you put your friend? Be aware of where you imagine them and how you imagine them. Be aware of the particular connections you make when you think of them.

Part III

GESTALT PRACTICE

Chapter 8

ASSESSMENT AND PLANNING

As we move into describing Gestalt practice, we need to pause briefly in order to invite you to think about your first meeting with your client and how to make a plan for your work together; a plan which can be flexible and constantly open to the changing needs of the moment and of the relationship. Perls (1947) says: 'As soon as the structure . . . is clear to the therapist, he should plan his course of action, but remain alert and elastic during the whole treatment.' Such a simple statement belies the difficulty faced by the Gestalt counsellor with her foundation of phenomenology, holism and respect for the individual. Perls' description of 'structure' implies diagnosis, a contentious area for some Gestalt practitioners. A premature or rigidly held assessment will deaden our perception and stereotype the individual without acknowledging his uniqueness and fluidity. Consequently, many have chosen to ignore diagnosis altogether for fear of losing the quality of the here-and-now moment.

However, most Gestalt practitioners see the value of assessment and diagnosis in order to plan for effective treatment. In a sense, anyway, we cannot *not* assess. As we saw earlier, humans are meaning-making creatures. They notice and they make sense of what they notice all the time. From the moment our client comes into the consulting room we will be paying attention to him, feeling about and reacting to him. This noticing contributes to our assessment. That assessment may then be shared with the client to assist in goal setting.

Assessment in Gestalt counselling is most useful if it is phenomenological (your own and your client's experience).

Phenomenological Assessment

●

Observable Contact Functions

Movement. How does your client move — stiffly or in a relaxed way? Does he make a lot of movements or remain still?
Voice. Loud or soft, distant or present, fluent or tentative?
Seeing. Does he make eye contact? Is his gaze steady or darting?
Hearing. Does he hear what you say easily? Does he hear correctly or appear to mishear?

Contact Boundary

How well does your client make contact with you? What sort of contact? Do you feel an immediate response from her or is she distracted and distant? How and when does she break contact?

Cycle of Experience

Does the client have clear sensations, which he recognizes? Can he mobilize energy to respond to his needs; can he make a plan and take action? Does he complete his action satisfactorily and then withdraw?
What interruptions to the cycle do you notice?
What unfinished business or fixed gestalts do you notice or does the client talk about?

Self and Environmental Support

What is the client's breathing like? Is it deep and relaxed, trusting both in the self and in the ability of the world to offer nourishment? Does she seem able to soothe and regulate her experience? Does she relax into the support of her chair? Does she refuse your feedback, or is she overdependent on it? Does she report having a supportive network of family or friends?

The Field

What life circumstances are impinging on the client at the

moment? What are the cultural, social or sexual implications of his situation?

Your Response

What feelings and images do you have in response to the client? Do you like him? Why? Try to allow your observations to be tentative. To say of someone, "He has an interruption at the appraisal stage of the cycle" has the effect of labelling a person in a fixed way. If we say, "He is interrupting...", it is an active mobile process which allows for change.

In addition to the broad assessment overview described above, there are some crucial specific questions which the counsellor needs to address. Why has the client come? What problems is she bringing and what does she want from counselling? How does what you notice in the assessment link with her areas of distress? What are the ways in which they impair her contact and functioning and which of them will become the focus of your work together?

In the appendices at the end of this book we have included two forms that the Gestalt counsellor may find useful in helping to conduct the initial assessment. One is an Assessment Checklist (Greenway, 1992) and the other is a set of Client Intake Sheets (Joyce, 1992). They offer more detailed suggestions about Gestalt assessment. You may wish to use them after the initial interview as a way of thinking about your client, and then add to them from time to time as other important information emerges. Be aware of what you notice, but do not try to make sense of it all within the session. Assessment should not interfere with your meeting with the client. It entails relating in an I–It mode, but only as a useful ground for the potential emergence of the I–Thou relationship. In Chapter 9 we describe 'bracketing', which stresses the importance of putting our judgements to one side.

Is Gestalt Counselling Suitable?

Gestalt has very powerful tools for heightening awareness, not the least of which is the work in the dialogue with its implicit demand for contact. Gestalt can put clients in touch with 'parts of themselves' that they did not previously know and loosen the restrictive bonds that people place on themselves through limited knowledge, habit or fear. Gestalt is sometimes called the 'solvent' which can dissolve the old rigid patterns of living in order to open up new options.

There are some people, however, for whom the full range of Gestalt counselling would not be appropriate or, at the very least, would need to be used with caution. These include the people for whom life is already too disorienting and disturbing. They often have a sense of fragmentation, of being lost or ungrounded. These people need glue, not solvent. They need to find a way of holding themselves together and taking an ordinary place in the world. This is not to say that Gestalt counselling is therefore unsuitable. Many Gestaltists work successfully with, for example, psychotic clients, basing their work on anxiety reduction, reality testing and the slow building of a relationship which encourages and supports their improving management of their lives. Awareness is increased slowly and confrontation is completely avoided. For further reading on this topic we recommend articles in the Spring 1979 edition of the *American Gestalt Journal* and the chapter by Harris in Edwin Nevis (ed), *Gestalt Therapy Perspectives and Applications* (1992). However, for the beginning Gestalt counsellor, this specialist work should not be undertaken without careful psychiatric supervision.

One can think about health as a continuum with perfectly healthy process in one direction and extreme disturbance in the other. We all lie somewhere along this continuum. None of us is perfectly healthy; we all have some sort of disturbances to our process at some times. A task of assessment is to find out where on the continuum a prospective client may lie, in order to be sure that they fall within the range of our competence and experience and also that they are likely to benefit from the approach we are using.

A full description of the different types of psychopathology you might encounter would not be appropriate here, so we are going to offer some basic guidelines to help you decide whether Gestalt counselling is suitable.

1　If your potential client has such severely impaired contact functions that they are not able to have some real meeting with you: that is to say, if their experiences are greatly outside the range of ordinariness — for instance, if they report seeing things which are not there or hearing things which you cannot hear; if they do not answer your questions meaningfully; if their language is jumbled or strange and you cannot make sense of it — they will probably not immediately benefit from Gestalt counselling. We suggest that in this case, at least in the first instance, your job, if possible, is to facilitate this person's receiving medical help. Perhaps later, with the continued support of the doctor, counselling which focuses predominantly on increased self-support may be helpful.

Mark is 19 and in his first year of college. His friend brings him to see the counsellor, as he has become increasingly distressed recently. At Mark's request, the friend accompanies him into the consulting room. Mark makes eye contact with the counsellor, although in an irregular way, and at first answers her questions appropriately. He says he is not enjoying college life because no-one likes him. When asked how he knows this, he at first says he can see it in their eyes. Then he says that he has heard people talking about him, although he was alone. The voices criticize him and describe him as scum, stupid, too small and so on. When the counsellor gently asks whether he might have been mistaken, or misunderstood what he heard, Mark becomes very agitated. Although it is a hot day, Mark is wearing a sweater and smells unwashed.

The counsellor suspects the onset of a psychosis and helps Mark to arrange an appointment with his doctor, who subsequently refers him to a psychiatrist.

2 If your potential client has some severe disturbance in contact functions and interruptions in the cycle of experience, yet has some meaningful contact with you and is able to think with you about the problem, it may be that medical help would still be of benefit. But this could be in conjunction with Gestalt counselling. Your supervisor will help you think how best to work with this client, and to decide whether any special measures for ensuring his safety would be relevant.

Jim is a 37-year-old accountant. He makes intermittent eye contact with the counsellor; his language is slow and flat, with long pauses between phrases; his appearance is somewhat unkempt; he interrupts the cycle of experience at appraisal as he talks obsessively about a problem. However, his words are clear and make sense to the counsellor; he is able to give an account of himself, including his history and why he has come. He is aware that his functioning is impaired.

Clare is a 45-year-old woman, married with three children who are growing up and starting to leave home. She stares at the ground and does not answer the counsellor's questions. She says that she cannot bear her life and she rambles incoherently as she twists her handkerchief in her fingers. She is painfully thin and there are huge dark circles under her eyes. She seems trapped in her own dark world. However, when the counsellor, as part of making her assessment, gently asks her to look at her, she does so. She is able to describe her life (her daily functioning, relationships and so on) and is able to say how long she has been depressed.

Both Jim and Clare were able to make use of Gestalt counselling, but Clare needed medication initially, in order to help her out of the trough of depression that she had been in for some eight months.

3   There is one other caveat that we would like to suggest to you. Always take your own feelings into account. For example, do not agree to work with a client if you feel frightened of them. It would not be fair on either of you. Even if you judge that your fear is a result of your own unfinished business rather than that of your client, you will still be unable to offer your best attention. Discuss with your supervisor the meaning of your fear.

Planning the Work

Once you have decided that Gestalt counselling is suitable for your potential client, you are free to think about treatment direction and 'negotiating consensus' (Zinker, 1977), which means agreeing the focus of your work together. If a counsellor and a client were to make an agreement to work in a purely Gestalt way, it would be that they should bring themselves as fully as possible to the here and now, to meet and explore anything and everything that emerges, to achieve mutuality of contact. However, clients rarely come with this aim in mind: they come with problems and difficulties with which they want the counsellor to help them. It is the counsellor's responsibility to hold the polarity between an approach which believes that ultimately growth and health come from the relationship of two individuals meeting without preconceived expectations or desires and, at the other pole, the client's need for help with a particular problem. In other words, on one hand there is the aim of a 'dialogic' meeting, with its natural flow between I–It and I–Thou moments; on the other, there is the necessity for a particular kind of I–It focusing on how a client may be contributing to their own difficulties.

Thus any plan for counselling cannot simply be a list of symptoms with how and in what order to treat them. It must be a subtle guide which is always available to negotiation. It is common to use the word 'journey' to describe the process of growth and change which is undertaken in the company of a counsellor or therapist. We prefer to see *life* as the journey and counselling as a part or stage of it. One can see counselling planning, therefore, as being two facilitators of this part of the journey: the map and the method of travel.

The Map

It is often said that we should not confuse the map with the territory. This is a good axiom to remember when planning a counselling journey. We must always be responsive to the actual 'territory' we encounter, being willing to take detours, make stopovers or even change the destination. We offer here an informal map of Gestalt counselling. But think of it like the maps that the children in Arthur Ransome's *Swallows and Amazons* made. They spent their summer camping and exploring the waterways and surrounding countryside. Their map started as an outline of the rivers and the coast and then they filled it in themselves as they explored it. They marked the marshy bits and the creeks, they marked the spot where they met the charcoal burners, and the place where the houseboat was moored. They named each place in a way that was meaningful to them. They did not use someone else's map because their experience was unique and it was theirs. The same applies to your treatment plan. Take the outline and fill it in with the unique details of the journey with your client. Use it to plot your adventure, rather than dictate it. Our map is simple. It contains three phases.

The First Phase

Arguably the most important task of the first phase of counselling is the building of a relationship of sufficient trust and commitment that the client can feel safe and supported enough to make the journey. The boundaries of time, place, fees and confidentiality are agreed and the work begins. Clients soon realize that they are expected to pay attention to themselves and respect themselves and the task of heightening awareness is under way. It is to be hoped that they also feel attended to, heard and understood. As the phase progresses, the exploration continues. The areas to be explored arise naturally out of the contact between the two people.

The client's task is to find out 'Who am I? How am I in the world?' Normally, it is not a phase concerned with change — unless there is an immediate crisis or problem that needs action — but with being oneself and expressing oneself. It is also concerned with developing healthy process and enough 'self-support' to go on to a deeper exploration and the possible challenging of old ways of being. Themes and patterns of thinking, feeling and behaving begin to emerge and are brought to awareness. Another important feature is that disowned parts of the person may be recognized, struggled with and integrated.

For some clients, this initial phase may be quite short. If the client makes good contact and is familiar with the notion of heightening awareness, he may move on swiftly. For some, however, it will take longer — weeks, months or longer. If a client habitually interrupts contact by projecting danger, he may take a considerable time to build a relationship in which he can trust the counsellor. If he is very blocked on the cycle at sensation and recognition, the process of heightening awareness will be slow.

The length of this phase will also depend on whether the client and counsellor have agreed a long- or short-term contract. Sometimes a client may choose to leave at the end of this phase. It may be that they came wanting to understand themselves better, to get help in making a decision or to mourn a bereavement. In this case their work will be completed. Indeed, at a suitable point in any stage of counselling, a client may choose to continue their journey without the counsellor as companion. At some future time they may decide to re-enter counselling for another stage.

The Second Phase

In the second phase of counselling, the task is to explore the themes that have emerged in more depth. Sometimes this may involve identifying and resolving unfinished business from the past. Gestalt counselling is present centred. It emphasizes the here and now. However, we do not only live in the present, we all have a past and a future. The aim of Gestalt counselling is not just to make today's figure lively: it is also to discover how yesterday's figures — our history (what Gordon Wheeler, 1991, calls 'ground structure') — are still affecting our present, and to look to the potential figures of our desired future and grow towards them. Clients may discover and challenge core beliefs about themselves, others and the world which underlie their disturbances in process. They may experiment with new options of behaviour. Continuing our analogy of the map, this stage involves going further into uncharted waters. Another metaphor of Gordon Wheeler's is relevant here. He describes feelings (1994) as the 'compass . . . they serve to *orient* us, to point us where we want to go (or away from where we don't want to go)'.

The second phase of counselling may also vary in length. The counsellor must be aware of whatever difficulties the client brought initially and ensure that the focus of the work addresses them. Together counsellor and client metaphorically explore the outline map they made and this provides the structure to the journey. The counsellor does not push the client to get an ocean-going boat and sail out to sea. If you have read *Swallows and Amazons*, you will know how singularly inappropriate and irrelevant that would be.

The Final Phase

This phase of the journey involves integration and practising of new ways of being and behaving. Some of the work done will need to be repeated or consolidated. The relationship between counsellor and client is characterized by an increase in authentic dialogue as both see the other as they really are, and can meet with mutuality of contact.

Gradually, issues of ending begin to be addressed. Client and counsellor sit down with the map and review with satisfaction where they have been. Sometimes it is necessary to revisit some parts of it. There is sadness at the ending of this particular part of life's journey as well as excitement at making plans for the future. For clients who experience difficulties towards the end of the cycle of experience — completion and withdrawal — this is a particularly important time and much vital work can be done. They are given the opportunity to do their ending differently, neither clinging on to the contact, nor breaking if off precipitately in an avoidance of the pain of separation. Ideally, they can reflect on what they have learned and achieved, express their feelings and prepare to leave. The counsellor will do the same. Then client and counsellor say goodbye.

The Method of Travel
●

The second facilitator of the journey is the method of travel used. The Swallows and Amazons used a combination of walking and small boats, sometimes with oars, sometimes with sails. The method chosen was of course relevant to the particular activity of the day, the weather, the depth of water, the task at hand. In Gestalt counselling, the method of travel is an approach which also, broadly speaking, has two elements or bands.

The first band involves using the phenomenological method in order to increase awareness and the ability to relate in the here and now, within the dialogic relationship which offers the authentic field in which further work can take place. It also involves supporting healthy functioning (as described above and in Chapter 11) and the development of self-support. These are approaches that you will use with all your clients, regardless of their particular problems and needs.

The second band involves the use of specific interventions designed to assist the client in achieving better understanding and awareness of herself, learning about or developing new options and exploring previously hidden parts of herself. Some of this overlaps with the first band, as these interventions will also, for example, increase self-support. These interventions are grouped under the heading of 'experiments'. This word is chosen because it underlines the philosophy that the Gestalt counsellor does not set out to *change* the client, but to meet her where she is and invite her to push the boundaries of her habitual way of being by experimenting. Experiments pay specific attention to interruptions to healthy functioning: fixed gestalts, unsatisfying completions, absences or difficulties in contact functions, and indeed any aspect of the client's functioning. The counsellor notices the figures and how they are related to the client's presenting problem. He may then choose from a number of Gestalt techniques in order to address the particular area — techniques which may be either to promote healthy functioning or to undo some pattern of living which is limiting the client. The choice of experiments will depend on the particular needs of the client, and their effectiveness will be linked to a number of variables, including timing, appropriateness and so on.

As you may imagine, the difference between the two bands is subtle and we have had to be quite arbitrary in our categorization. In practice, the Gestalt counsellor flows easily between the two bands as she follows the pace and the energy of the client: phenomenological exploring develops smoothly into an experiment as the work progresses. However, it is useful to consider them separately in order to become more aware of what the counsellor does. In the next five chapters, we will describe these two bands in depth.

Chapter 9

PHENOMENOLOGY AND AWARENESS

Terry Cooper (personal communication, 1980) likens the counselling process to one in which the client brings his experience as if it were a precious possession. He reaches out and offers it to the counsellor. Then, he says that there are several sorts of counsellor. There is the one who takes the offering, looks at it meaningfully, then puts it in her pocket 'for later'. There is the one who takes it, twists it into a different shape and hands it back, unrecognizable. Then there is the counsellor who takes it, stares at it, then tosses it up in the air in alarm, as if it were a hot potato. The good counsellor is the person who takes the offering respectfully and looks at it carefully from various angles. She may hold it out to the client in order that he also may see it from different angles. She then hands it back to its owner.

Of course this is a simplified analogy. The way the client and the counsellor are relating is the field in which they make sense of experience and the experience itself will be affected by this field. The offering cannot be completely unchanged in the process. However, we find it a powerful and useful metaphor for the most fundamental form of Gestalt counselling.

In Part II we described briefly the philosophy of existentialism and phenomenology which are the backbone of Gestalt theory. In this chapter, we look at the way phenomenology translates into practice. Remember that we described phenomenology as the subjective experience of 'what is'. It is the study of the client's feelings, meaning making and truth. Before we go on to describe the phenomenological method, we invite you to do an exercise. Look at the picture of the man on the opposite page. Write down at least eight things that come into your mind as you look at him. Do not stop to examine your responses, simply list them as they occur to you. How many of them are pure description? For

instance, you may have noticed that he is grey-haired, clean-shaven and so on. Probably many of your responses, however, involve some interpretation on your part. You may have described him as grumpy, thoughtful, severe, peaceful, friendly-looking. You may have noticed that he seems to be meeting your gaze, or something about the way he dresses. You might be interested to ask a friend or colleague to do the same exercise. Do they notice the same things or do they notice different ones? Are the interpretations they put on the things they notice the same as yours? Probably not.

What do you notice about your responses to the picture? Do they confirm or reveal anything about you? For instance, do you have biases in your expectations of people relating to gender? Are you the sort of person who describes someone but does not 'get a feel' of them? Are you, on the contrary, someone who quickly thinks about someone in relational terms — how they might behave to you and you to them?

The exercise illustrates very simply some of the concepts we have written about in Part II of this book. We have our individual ways of noticing and of interpreting what we notice. They are based on individual, social and cultural learning experiences of which we are only partly aware, as well as on situational factors and the mood we are in. As Ernesto Spinelli (1989) puts it: 'far from being objective, our perceptions of others typically contain variables which more correctly define and describe psychological factors in the make-up of the perceiver rather than point out accurate, universally shared "facts" about the perceived'.

The phenomenology of our clients is the way *they* see themselves, other people and the world. Our first job as a counsellor is to help them become aware of how they perceive the world. Carl Rogers (1951) pointed out that a person cannot move psychologically from their position until they have been fully accepted in that position. The truth of this is easy to confirm. Think of a time when you had a fierce argument with a partner or friend. The chances are that you had different viewpoints and that what you felt most angry and frustrated about is that your view was not being taken seriously. Normally, we do not need the other person to *agree* with us (though that is nice too!) — we need to be *heard*. When our friend sees our point of view, if they can say "I see, so the way you feel is this . . ." or "So what you experienced is that . . .", we immediately become calmer. We feel understood, and we are more ready to hear another point of view.

Clients need us to listen and to understand; they need to listen and to understand themselves. They become aware of who they are. Then, paradoxically, they will be open to growth. We, as counsellors, must put aside our own perceptions, biases, interpretations and value judgements in order to be fully open to the client's true experience. In this way, we can invite our clients to raise their awareness in a spirit of interested investigation rather than one of labelling and judgement. In order to follow the phenomenological method, the counsellor practises three techniques or attitudes.

Epoche or Bracketing

Epochē is a Greek word meaning a stop, check or pause. It comes from ep-echein, 'to have or to hold'. In counselling terms this means that we are willing temporarily to hold to one side all our own values, prejudices, understandings and priorities — in short, everything which colours our experience. This is in order to be able to meet the client's experience 'without memory and without desire' (Bion, 1959). Later we may choose to share something we have held aside, if the time seems right. In practice, of course, it would be impossible to bracket off all our perceptions and judgements. They are too much a part of us. But, as Gestalt counsellors, this is what we aim to do. When our client says, "I am expecting a baby", we do not automatically assume that this is a happy event; we may say, "How do you feel about that?" Our client may be scared, shocked, angry or excited. Similarly, when our client says, "The bus driver shouted at me", we do not assume that she feels upset in the way that we might. She may have felt invigorated. We wait to see what emerges.

Thus the counsellor's exploration should not be interpretation or association. It is not asking the question Why? or What for? It is asking questions like "What are you doing now?", "How are you holding your body?", "What are you feeling?", "What are you saying to yourself as you do that?", "What does that do for you?", "What happens next?", "Do you want to be doing that?", "What else could you do?"

The following is an example of a counsellor practising bracketing as his client, Emily, describes a scene at work. She says that her boss is abusing her. The counsellor has an immediate picture of a tyrannical, balding man — somewhat like his own father — and feels angrily sympathetic. However, he brackets off his reaction.

COUNSELLOR: What's that like for you?
EMILY: It's funny really, because she is in a wheelchair and could not hit me, but I feel terribly scared.
COUNSELLOR: So you think it's odd of you to be scared.
EMILY: I suppose I do. She shouts and screams so.
COUNSELLOR: And what are you frightened of?
EMILY: Well, I'm frightened... Actually, I'm frightened that she will die, like my grandmother did when she was shouting one day. I never realized until now that it was Grandma she reminded me of.

Every one of the counsellor's interventions involved some bracketing. There was his initial reaction when he imagined his father, then his own view that shouting in any form is unpleasant. The he bracketed his assumption that Emily was frightened for her own safety. By phenomenological enquiry, he was able to facilitate Emily's understanding of a deeper cause of her fear.

Description

The second rule of the phenomenological method is to describe rather than explain. Having bracketed our assumptions and values, we are then faced with another tendency, vital to human living, yet restricting in this context. It is the tendency to make meaning and explain what is happening rather than simply to experience it. An example is that of a woman sitting in a deckchair, full in the sun. She is squinting up her eyes. A description is simply that: she is squinting up her eyes. An explanation is that she is protecting them from the glare. However, if we release ourselves from the limitations of our first perceptions (remember the figures in Chapter 6) there are many possible explanations for her behaviour. She may be involved in thinking about a puzzling dilemma; she may be experimenting to see what the trees look like through half-closed eyes; she may be exercising her face muscles.

Following the rule of description we avoid putting any interpretation on things and allow the client to explore their own phenomenology. We may draw their attention to what we notice about them and invite them to notice themselves in the same way and find out what is *their* explanation. And we do not look for the obscure or subtle; we look at the obvious. Clarkson and Mackewn (1993) quote Perls as saying, "I have frequently discovered that the obvious has been taken for granted not only by the patient, but by the therapist as well."

Gestalt counsellors are aware that fixed gestalts, though originally formed as creative adjustments to situations in the past, are no longer in the past. They are in the present: 'The uppermost surface of our behaviour is, in fact, the expression of our present dominant need and of our unfinished business' (Clarkson and Mackewn, 1993). By noticing, naming and exploring 'the obvious', we help people become aware of those fixed gestalts and restore the ability to respond creatively and flexibly to life's experience. Sometimes, of course, it will be necessary for the client to talk about the past and even relive parts of it in order to complete unfinished business. However, often the counsellor's approach will be to bring these old patterns of behaving, thinking and feeling into the foreground where they can be experienced in the present as conscious activities for which the client can take responsibility. The counsellor does this by noticing a tone of voice or gesture, a facial expression, the use of a word, a choice of clothes or job or car and so on, and commenting on it. All these are interventions which are descriptive in quality and allow the client to explore himself fully in the present.

Horizontalism

This means that everything in your client's field is given the same importance as everything else. It is also known as equalization. In a way it is a form of bracketing, as it involves the counsellor suspending her powers of prioritizing and selection. The client's experience is approached as if it were a jigsaw puzzle. Each piece is equally important in making the whole, even though it may be 'just' a piece of sky rather than part of a person's face.

The value of horizontalism in counselling is that it allows both counsellor and client to look at the whole. Everything is relevant, from the client's tiny finger movements as she talks, to something in the wider field, like the fact that she has bought a new pair of gloves. Also important may be the parts that the client does not mention, for instance what she was doing for the hour before her mother came to visit, or how she felt as she prepared to make a difficult telephone call. A client's fear of horses in seen differently in the context of her living in the city centre than if right next door to a riding stables.

For some weeks, Betty has been talking about her lack of confidence. Today she seems listless and unable to focus on anything.

COUNSELLOR: I notice you are wearing a red sweater today. I have never seen you in red before.

BETTY: Oh, I never wear it. It was because everything else was in the wash.

COUNSELLOR: You looked quite energetic as you said that.

BETTY: Well, I guess... actually, you know, I had just received that letter from my mother. And I thought, 'Mum would hate this, she'd say it was too loud' and I put it on.

COUNSELLOR: So the choice is significant.

BETTY: [*giggles*] I think it is. I think I wanted to defy her. I like red and I like wearing it.

Betty goes on to talk animatedly about wanting to stand up to her mother.

Another important value in horizontalism is that it allows client and counsellor to focus on their responses to each other which may at first seem irrelevant or incongruous. In particular, they may notice and explore the phenomena of transference and counter-transference. Transference occurs when the client 'transfers' onto the counsellor the thoughts, feelings and reactions that they had towards someone in the past. They 'put someone's face' onto the counsellor. Counter-transference refers to the responses of the counsellor to the client. These may be the natural responses of one human being to another, but they may have other implications. They may be reactions triggered by the force of the client's transference or the resonances with the client's unspoken feelings. They may also, of course, be the counsellor's own transferring of past relationships onto the present. Feelings of transference and counter-transference which are not amenable to up-dating in the here and now are indications of unfinished business and fixed gestalts.

Peter looks resentfully at his counsellor as he describes how unfair his wife is being.

COUNSELLOR: You are sounding angry and I am feeling very sad at this moment. I wonder if you are sad.

[Peter's face softens and grows heavy.]

PETER: You're right, I am very sad. I don't know what to do when I am sad.

Examples of the Phenomenological Method

●

In practice the three rules of the phenomenological method are interdependent. In the following examples the counsellor uses bracketing, description, horizontalism and also her own phenomenology to heighten the client's awareness. The client is talking about differences in her marriage.

JEAN: The more I think about him the sadder I feel. I keep wishing I hadn't said what I did and I just want to cry all the time.

COUNSELLOR: You tell me you are sad, then you look at me and smile.

JEAN: Do I?

COUNSELLOR: Weren't you aware of it?

JEAN: No I wasn't, you see I ... there, I just did it then — I smiled at you as I started to speak.

COUNSELLOR: What are you aware of as you smile?

JEAN: I'm thinking that I don't want to upset you ... umm . . . I think I want to reassure you that I'm all right really.

COUNSELLOR: You look quite anxious as you say that, and there is energy in your voice.

JEAN: Yes, I feel anxious. It's silly but I'm afraid you might get depressed . . . oh, yes [*sighs*] . . . like my mother ... if ever I had a problem, she suffered more than I did and often was deeply depressed. I learned to pretend that everything was fine. Pretend and pretend. And you know what? I do the same with Rick.

COUNSELLOR: And I notice as you talk to me now you have stopped those little smiles.

In this example, the client realized how she projected her mother onto the counsellor and, with a combination of introjection and retroflection, interrupted her healthy self process.

In the following example, counsellor and client explore Bill's

105

lack of energy at the appraisal and mobilization stage of the gestalt cycle.

BILL:	I'm not getting what I want out of this group.
COUNSELLOR:	What is it that you want?
BILL:	Well that's it . . . I don't know what I want . . . I want the group to help me.
COUNSELLOR:	I notice the position you are lying in right now. How is that for you?
BILL:	Well, I'm almost lying flat with just my head propped on the cushion. I guess I'm 'slumped'.
COUNSELLOR:	And I notice you are breathing very shallowly.
BILL:	That's true. It's actually hard to breathe deeply in this position. Actually I feel rather like a beached walrus.
COUNSELLOR:	You look sad at the idea of being a walrus on a beach.
BILL:	I feel bad when you say that — and sort of scared. That would mean I couldn't move easily. I'd be waiting for the tide to come in before I could have my freedom.
COUNSELLOR:	Freedom?
BILL:	To move . . . to be what I want to be. [*Bill looks thoughtful*] But even walruses move on their own. They can get down to the sea . . . I need to go down to the sea . . . to go where I want and do what I want.
COUNSELLOR:	And, as you say that, you have started to sit up and gesture with your arms. What is going on for you now?
BILL:	I want to stand up and walk around.

In the last example, Dave is interrupting the cycle at the sensation–recognition stage.

DAVE:	I don't know what to talk about. I feel flat and low today.
COUNSELLOR:	Your voice sounds low and flat. Your body looks quite tense and restless. How do you feel in your body?

DAVE: Yes, I feel restless. I don't know why. I feel restless and agitated.

COUNSELLOR: Now you're frowning and your voice sounds quite angry.

DAVE: You're right. I do feel angry. Actually, I think I've been feeling angry ever since yesterday when my boss ticked me off for something that was nothing to do with me.

COUNSELLOR: You are very energized now. The whole atmosphere in the room has changed.

DAVE: I do feel angry. I think I will go and speak to him tomorrow and explain.

Exercises

1 Surfacing assumptions
Return to the picture on page 99. Imagine that the man's name is Augustus Bennet-French. What new or altered assumptions do you make about him?

Now imagine that he is a doctor; a dustman; an accountant; a Gestalt practitioner. What effect does this have on your interpretation of this picture?

With a partner, take it in turns to talk about something that is interesting or worrying you. The listener limits any interventions to clarifying the belief system of the talker. Use phrases like "So you believe that ...", "It sounds as if you feel ...", "It's important to you that ...", and so on. This is not an exercise in phenomenology but in heightening your awareness of the number of assumptions and values that are embedded in everything we say. Noticing the assumptions we make about someone else's values can be very revealing. For the purposes of this exercise, practise clarifying the belief even when you are sure you know it or if you wholeheartedly agree with it. The exercise is somewhat stilted. However, it will show you how much of our conversation comes out of a personal frame of reference. Here is an example to demonstrate the exercise.

JO: So I was driving along at between 35 and 40 miles per hour.

JIM: It sounds as if accuracy is important to you.

JO: Yes, it is. And there was this awful man tearing along in the outside lane doing at least 80.

JIM: You thought he was wrong to go that fast.

JO: Well, it was faster than the speed limit.

JIM: Your belief about what is wrong is justified by the law. So you think that breaking the law is wrong?

JO: On the roads, I do.

JIM: So you think some laws are OK to break and some aren't?

JO: I guess so. And there were children in the car.

JIM: So it sounds as if you think that the safety of children is more important than that of adults.

JO: Well, yes. They can't take care of themselves, can they? They rely on grown-ups.

JIM: So if a person can't take care of themselves, then their safety becomes more important.

JO: I guess I've always believed that the needs of the vulnerable were more important.

And so on. Play with this exercise and see what you discover about yourselves. With clients, of course, it is not appropriate to interrupt at every turn in order to clarify their beliefs. Sometimes you will need to make provisional assumptions which you will need to change or confirm at some future point.

2   Description
Stay sitting as you are, reading this book. Now describe yourself as you might be seen by someone else. Take care not to explain or interpret.

Do the same exercise with a figure on television, the man opposite you on the bus, and so on.

With a partner, practise reflective listening as they talk, confining your description to the content of what they say and of what you see or hear.

3   Horizontalism
What is the most significant thing about you that you are aware

of at this moment? Now focus on your left foot. How does it feel? What position is it in? Imagine that your left foot is the most significant part of you right now. What are you telling yourself with your foot?

With a partner, take it in turns to talk and listen, commenting on anything you notice, whether it seems relevant or not. Give feedback as the speaker about how you experience the exercise.

4 Combining the elements

With a partner or with clients, practise all three elements of the phenomenological method. Pay attention to what your client is bringing but also specifically try to bracket your assumptions and open your awareness to the variety and richness of their present experience.

As you practise, you will find that your attention is drawn this way and that until some compelling figure emerges from the ground. You and your client explore it. Your attention rests with that figure: is it vivid and new, is it completed in a satisfying way or is it fixed or interrupted? What does the client reveal to you and himself in relation to the figure? Now withdraw your attention from that figure and again be open to the next compelling emergent figure.

Chapter 10

WORKING IN THE DIALOGUE

Yontef & Simkin (1989) say, 'Awareness and dialogue are the two primary therapeutic tools in Gestalt.' In Part II of this book we described the counselling relationship in Gestalt and the healing for the client that can take place through this contact. How then do we practise offering this sort of relationship? Martin Buber's (1984) three essential elements of an I–Thou dialogue are the qualities which, ideally, the counsellor will bring to the counselling relationship. This will not mean that their goal is to be in an I–Thou meeting all the time. It would not be possible. As Hycner (1990) says, 'To try and "force" an I–Thou relationship is to be guilty of a modern "hubris".' What is strived for is 'an approach, an attitude, an orientation, an outlook . . . the willingness . . . to submit to the "between"' (*ibid*).

Presence

As the name implies, presence means being fully in the here and now, ready to be alive to every facet of the moment. In relation to dialogue this involves the willingness to meet the client honestly, to be aware of our thoughts, feelings and behaviours in response to them and to the relationship we are developing. The emphasis is upon being authentic rather than assuming a caring role or attempting to be neutral. We respect our own selves as well as our clients and are ready to know ourselves. The openness and acceptance that we demonstrate invite a similar openness in our clients. In Chapter 3, we described a moment of real connection between two women at a railway station. It is our experience that this sort of encounter happens *only* when we are wholly in the present, and willing to give ourselves unreservedly to the meeting in that moment. In counselling, there are frequent changes from I–It to I–Thou and back again. We aim to be present and available throughout the session.

John walks into the counselling room and sits down. The counsellor sits and focuses herself on the two of them sitting together. She is aware of her feelings of warmth for John, whom she has known for some time. She is aware of the peacefulness of the room, and the comfortable feel of the chair in which she sits. She looks at John. His face looks drawn and sad to the counsellor. She feels concern for him. She waits for him to speak.

Inclusion

This means that the counsellor, being present, attempts to enter the phenomenological world of the client, see it through the client's eyes and then offer *confirmation* that the client has been 'apprehended and acknowledged' in their whole being (Buber, 1965). We try to experience what it is like to be that person, with all their thoughts, feelings and attitudes. Some experiences, such as loss or loneliness, are common to everyone. We can resonate with such experiences, easily and immediately, even if the circumstances are very different. This helps us to step inside our client's world. However, the cautious counsellor remembers to check the accuracy of their resonance with the client, as different people have very different responses to the same event. Sometimes the client's situation is so different from our own life experience that we have no match. However, human feelings are universal and there are always some aspects or dynamics of a situation that we can imagine and identify with as we pay close attention to the client's account and see the world through his eyes.

At the same time we retain a sense of our self as a separate person. We allow ourselves to be affected by the client while remaining aware that we are the Thou or It to our client's I, as well as vice versa. We are willing to put aside our own values and prejudices in order fully to respect the truth of the other. We want to stress that inclusion does not mean total immersion in the experience of the client. We cannot feel our clients' feelings for them or think their thoughts for them. What we can do is empathize with their experience. It is as if we move briefly into their experiential world — enough to understand it — and then step back into ourselves. This process of connection and separation can be so fast as to seem simultaneous.

Looking at the floor and speaking in a low voice, John starts to talk about his loneliness. His wife died three months ago and, although he is coping with the day-to-day tasks of living, they seem to have no meaning for him. He says that he either feels deeply sad or he feels completely empty. When he goes out, he finds it hard to see other people going on with their lives as usual. It is odd to him that for the rest of the world nothing has changed. The counsellor responds to his experience of loss and alienation. She can imagine what it might be like to be in John's shoes. She feels sad, and also has the sense that John is a long way away from her. She expresses her empathy for John and how moved she feels. Then she says, "It sounds as if you don't feel as if you belong in the world any more." Tears come to John's eyes and he looks at the counsellor for the first time. "That's exactly how I feel." They look at each other for a moment and for that moment John's sadness is shared.

Genuine Communication

Being present and inclusive, we then experience a response to our clients which is immediate and based in our own phenomenology. The sharing of this experience becomes an open and honest communication with our clients. We must be willing to communicate some of our thoughts and feelings, even when they may not immediately seem to be sympathetic. In this way we are in a real relationship with another person: we are not just a mirror or an interpreter.

This does not mean that we will necessarily say everything of which we become aware. For instance, if we, with our training and experience, notice something about our clients before they do, it may be appropriate to allow the client to bring this to their own awareness at their own pace. Nor would we interrupt our client to share every response when this would mean getting in the way of their unfolding process. The aim is to communicate whatever we think will further the genuineness of the meeting and facilitate the growth of the client. Another way of looking at this would be: communicate anything which, *if not said*, would get in the way of the meeting. It is a delicate task, for a counsellor's job is not only to accept and be with the client where they are, but also to be with them at their growing edge — *confirming* their potential.

Being present and genuinely communicating our experience may mean reporting our feeling of irritation or telling a client that we have been distracted from their story by a particular mannerism. It may mean sharing the fact that we have started to feel unaccountably sad while our client was talking, even though we do not know why or how this is relevant. We are willing to take the risk of putting our experience into the 'between' of the relationship without controlling the outcome, but with an openness to meeting and being met. We move towards the client and invite the client to move towards us in a spirit of genuine and open exploration. We accept what *is* rather than what we may think *should* be.

Later in the session, as John describes his wife's funeral, the counsellor becomes aware that she has noticed John pulling at the neck of his sweater several times. She begins to feel constricted and finds herself hoping that the session is nearly over.

COUNSELLOR: This may be quite unconnected to your experience, but I notice that, for some reason, I keep thinking about getting away.

JOHN: I wanted to get away from the church. Isn't that terrible? But I did. I wanted to shout out, "Let's get it over with."

The three elements of dialogue in counselling are interdependent. We flow between them in a constantly moving process with our clients as we attend to them and their story, let ourselves be aware of our response and find a way of sharing that. 'Counsellors honour and enter the client's subjective world, accepting and confirming them as they currently are. At the same time [they] are trained to stay in touch with themselves sufficiently to know and judiciously show themselves, rather than act "as if" they were something else' (Mackewn, 1994). The following illustrations of working in the dialogue demonstrate that flow.

Mary starts to describe how unconfident she feels most of the time and how anxious she is about 'doing the wrong thing'. She has particular distress at work, where she starts to feel anxious whenever her boss walks into the room, but she says she feels nervous with anybody whom she sees as in authority. The counsellor asks who she sees as being 'in authority' and Mary answers, with a little laugh, "Almost anybody, really. I'm afraid they're going to criticize me."

COUNSELLOR: Do you see me as someone who will criticize you?

MARY: Yes, I do.

COUNSELLOR: How do you feel with me right now?

MARY: I feel anxious — my stomach is all knotted up and I'm thinking, "She thinks I'm silly, I'm so stupid..."

COUNSELLOR: I have a suggestion. Are you willing to say that to me?

MARY: You think I'm stupid. [*She looks away*] It's hard to look at you and say that.

COUNSELLOR: You find it difficult to look at me?

MARY: Yes, I'm frightened of seeing your criticism in your face.

COUNSELLOR: How are you imagining my face at this moment?

MARY: Angry and cold, with your eyebrows in a frown and your mouth all hard as if you were getting ready to shout at me.

COUNSELLOR: That *does* sound frightening.

(The counsellor resonates with Mary's feeling of anxiety and simultaneously is aware of feeling uncomfortable with the powerful position Mary perceives her to be in.)

COUNSELLOR: There are two things going on for me now. You fear that I am critical, and I can see how frightening that is for you. But at the same time, while you stay feeling frightened, you break contact with me by looking away, and you won't find out if what you believe is true or not.

MARY: Find out? . . . oh yes, I see, I am frightening myself

	with what I imagine you are looking like and what you are thinking. I could check. (*Looks at counsellor*)
COUNSELLOR:	What are you seeing?
MARY:	Your face. It isn't as I thought [*smiles*] . . . what *are* you thinking of me?
COUNSELLOR:	At this moment I am thinking how much more confident you look. Your body seemed to relax as you looked at me.
MARY:	I don't feel frightened now. I am pleased that I risked looking at you.

In this example, Mary starts off by relating in the I–It mode. She is not seeing the counsellor as another whole person. This is often the case with our clients, who may be very involved with the problems they are bringing and not free to make contact with us. Here the counsellor remains present with her in an I–Thou attitude. The counsellor practises inclusion by allowing herself to understand Mary's experience; then, by sharing some of her own responses and thoughts, she offers the opportunity for contact which Mary is willing to take. It is interesting to note that both Mary and Betty (example in the previous chapter) had difficulty in meeting the counsellor's eyes, but the meaning of that difficulty was different.

The following example illustrates the result of the counsellor being in the I–It mode and the change which occurred when she became more inclusive. Michael had been seeing the counsellor for three sessions, recommended by his doctor, whom he had consulted about his stress-related symptoms. At each session he talked with scarcely a pause and in rather a loud voice, without leaving any space for the counsellor to say anything. His manner seemed to the counsellor to be rather arrogant and domineering, and although she surmised that he might also be nervous, she had difficulty in retaining that understanding as time after time he responded to her comments with a slightly supercilious glance and continued his monologue. The counsellor began to try to find ways of telling him how she was experiencing him.

MICHAEL:	. . . and of course we had to make 26 people redundant. That's all part of the job, one just has to do it,

but I expect someone like you will say that I must have been stressed by that. My friend, Lois, who is a counsellor, says that I must feel as if I am overwhelmed sometimes, but one has a job to do and —

COUNSELLOR: I was wondering —

MICHAEL: But the important thing is that we concentrate here on the problem. I must get to the root of things quickly and move on . . . (*much more of the same*)

COUNSELLOR: I am beginning to feel over —

MICHAEL: I thought you would say that. Lois always says that she tells her clients what she is feeling . . . but I think we should look at the problem. How are we going to get rid of these stress symptoms? You see, in my job I . . .

(And so on. The counsellor began to feel completely unseen by her client, and decided that she needed to say something clever — or at least something that Lois had not thought of — in order to attract Michael's attention.)

COUNSELLOR: You seem to live your life a lot according to what you think you *ought* to do.

MICHAEL: You see sometimes one calls a fellow into the office and . . .

COUNSELLOR: You often say "one" when you are talking about yourself. Would you be willing to experiment with saying "I" and notice if you feel differently?

MICHAEL: Oh, ha ha! Yes, Lois says that to her clients. I do say "one" a lot. Well, as I say . . .

Things changed only when the counsellor stopped competing for control. Michael was talking about how he tried to do things properly, his various responsibilities and how he always noticed the details that were not perfect. He said with a laugh, "You could say I'm pretty hard on myself." Suddenly, the counsellor saw the tension in his body and heard the anxiety in his voice. She understood how much he feared disapproval — including, she realized, *her* disapproval. At the same moment she saw who he could be. She could imagine his body relaxing, his gaze meeting hers in a confident manner. The dialogue they could have. Then she felt a wave of warmth for the stressed person before her. Gently, but from her heart, she said, "Yes, you really are hard on yourself." Michael stopped and looked at her directly for what seemed like the first time. He said, "Thank you" and his eyes filled with tears.

Their relationship deepened from that moment. The counsellor realized how, in focusing on the fact that Michael did not 'see' her, she had managed to do the same thing to him. She was relating from an I–It position and she had omitted to see and hear his experience as she tried to get him to be something other than who he was. It must have felt to Michael like yet another person who wanted him to 'do better'. No wonder he did not want to listen. Her moment of inclusion was a moment of I–Thou meeting.

To read more about the dialogue in Gestalt counselling, in addition to the texts mentioned, we recommend *Developing Gestalt Counselling* (Mackewn, forthcoming) in which an integration is made with Gelso and Carter's (1985) components of the counselling relationship.

Exercises

●

For Yourself

1 Presence
Next time you are talking with a friend, let yourself take a moment to be aware of where you are. Put other thoughts out of your mind, whether they are things from the past with which you are still preoccupied or plans or worries about the future. Allow yourself to bring all of your awareness into the now. Notice your body position and your breathing. You may want to shift your position so that you feel well supported. Notice any sensations within your body. Now look at your friend. (Though this has taken several lines to write, it need only take a second or two.) Notice any changes in your attitude to the encounter with your friend.

2 Inclusion
When listening to someone telling their story (whether it is a friend or even someone on the television) let yourself fully imagine what it might be like to be that person in the situation they

are describing. How does your experience alter? Now let yourself live for a few moments as if you were in the shoes of that person without any comment or opinions coming from your own experience.

Ask a trusted friend or fellow trainee to engage with you in an exercise. Ask them to tell you about something that has happened recently in their lives. Practise checking in a variety of ways that you understand their experience. For example: (a) by summarizing the salient facts of the situation that you have heard. When your friend says, "My boss said that I could take my holiday from Friday but now he's asked me to go to a meeting on Monday and I don't know if I should say something about it", you might respond with "You don't know whether to confront your boss or not"; (b) by reflecting your friend's feelings with "It sounds as if you're anxious about the idea of confronting your boss"; (c) by commenting on the values or beliefs inherent in your friend's statement with "I get the impression that you think people should keep the agreements they make" or "You're not sure whether you have the right to confront your boss" or "It sounds as though you don't want to believe that your boss might have made a mistake."

Allow yourself to resonate with your friend's experience and then notice how you feel in response to them.

3 Genuine communication

Again ask the help of a trusted friend or fellow trainee. Listen to an account of their experience. (a) Notice your emotions, thoughts and sensations as they talk, and share them regularly without stopping to analyse or inhibit them: for instance, "I feel excited as you say that . . . I feel rather sad now . . . I feel less engaged with you now . . . I feel a bit scared in response to that." (b) Notice your friend's manner of expression and comment upon what you see: for instance, "I noticed that when you talked about your spoiled holiday plans, you made a fist with your hands, but now, as you talk about whether to speak to him, your arms are hanging slack and your voice has dropped."

Experiment with noticing and then letting go of your passing thoughts or responses, sharing only those which recur or remain in your awareness. For instance, you may notice that you feel irritated with your friend's hesitation, then, having let go of this, begin to empathize with his dilemma. You have a few transitory impressions: your friend's tie isn't straight; a squirrel runs past the window. You become aware, as your friend sits helplessly, that you are experiencing some anxiety. You continue to feel slightly anxious in spite of attempting to let go of this, so you share your feeling.

With Clients

Developing these aspects of the counselling relationship with your clients clearly cannot be done in the form of an exercise but only within the genuine face-to-face encounter. For this reason we suggest that the practice of the above exercises with friends and fellow trainees be carried out extensively prior to working with clients until you feel that you have a real sense of what the dialogue involves. When working with clients, offering them your full presence and inclusion will probably be the greatest gift you can give them. As for what you communicate of your own experience, remember to check before you speak that you are doing so from a respectful position and that the expression of your thoughts or feelings is in the service of the client and with 'dialogic intention', and not for relief of your own unfinished business.

A Last Word about the Relationship

You may notice, as you put this approach into practice, that there are differences in the way your clients relate to you. Some may talk easily about themselves, not appearing to need any response from you. Some seem to crave understanding or empathy but do not respond to other interventions. Others, on the contrary, seem to be more interested in hearing your comments.

In this book we have been describing the importance of contact and asking you to notice the ways that your client may interrupt their experience and their contact with you. Bringing this to the attention of your client is part of a counsellor's job. You ask yourself certain questions. Is the client who talks without wanting your response avoiding contact with you and indeed with himself? Is the client who desperately needs you to understand her showing an inability to trust her own feelings or perhaps an un-willingness to deal with difference? Is the client who wants your opinion avoiding thinking for himself about what he wants or be-lieves and trying to shift responsibility for his actions onto you? It may well be that the manner of making contact reveals much.

However, it may also be that these phenomena reflect a valid and healthy need. At various stages of the counselling process, your client may have different needs of your attention. Some people find it useful to think about child developmental stages and needs in relation to this issue. We may hypothesize that, at a particular stage in their growth, the client did not receive the appropriate relationship or received it inadequately, so that there is still a developmental need that forms part of the unfinished business that they bring.

This may be the need to be met emotionally — to receive the 'affective attunement', as Stern (1985) and others describe it. This is the way to meet the preverbal child. Alternatively, it may be the need for help in naming and verbalizing experiences, or thinking about them and planning for what they want. It may be the client's need to 'do it myself', which in the counselling room may translate as working something out for themselves, with minimal intervention, in order to achieve a sense of power in their own lives. Or it may be the echo of the three- or four-year-old — chattering excitedly about themselves and what they have done, figuratively trying on different identities as they explore themselves to find out who they are and who they want to be. In this case, they will need nothing but interested appreciation from the counsellor, who will be careful not to limit them with 'guid-ing' comments. And so on.

There is an implication of this framework for the dialogue. Before commenting on a client's seeming lack of interest in your responses, reflect whether perhaps your *presence* as an interested witness is all that is needed. When they are struggling for words, it may be that emotional *inclusion* is sufficient and that cognitive understanding misses them, precisely because there are no words for the experience. At other times affective attunement would be irrelevant because your client needs you to name what you are hearing in order for them to understand themselves.

There are times when *communication*, however genuine, could have the effect of interrupting the client's need to explore on their own, or simply to tell you their story. And then there are times when great excitement will come from exploring together in the give and take of the dialogue. As you offer yourself to the meeting, be aware that *confirmation* is a vital part of what a counsellor offers. We are confirming the client's wholeness and that confirmation may be of different aspects of the individual at different times.

The reader who is interested in these ideas about developmental stages may read more about them in Stern (1985), in Levin (1974), Mahler *et al* (1975) or Erikson (1950). However, a detailed knowledge is not necessary if you are working fully in the dialogue. If you give your complete and respectful attention to the client, if you are willing to respond to them, and then notice whether your responses were helpful, you will be able to discover what your client needs from you at a particular time. If you are not sure that what you are doing is useful to your client, you can ask.

Chapter 11

PROMOTING HEALTHY PROCESS

In the previous two chapters, we have been emphasizing the importance of meeting the client without any investment other than to be with 'what is'. However, we believe that the counsellor has certain responsibilities to encourage and nurture specific aspects of the client's functioning. We offer five areas in which this is the case.

Integrating Mind and Body

Perls *et al* (1951) recognized that people are 'unified organisms', part of and in relation with their environments. He was rather scathing of psychiatry and those psychotherapies which insisted upon viewing only separate parts — mind or body, thoughts or feelings, being or doing, person or environment — rather than a holistic approach to the person. He wrote, 'We believe further that the "mental–physical" or "mind–body" split is a totally artificial one, and that to concentrate on either term in this false dichotomy is to preserve neurosis, not to cure it' (Perls, 1976). The Gestalt counsellor helps the client to reclaim and reunify the conceptual separations they may have made both in their view of themselves and in relation to their environmental field. They encourage clients, stuck in the habit of 'thinking about' or analysing situations, to refocus on their bodies and emotions in order to integrate them as natural parts of healthy living. Even as we wrote the previous sentence, we were aware how the very phrases are suggesting a dichotomy between mind, body and feelings. It is almost impossible to use words about ourselves without doing so. Despite this paradox, we invite you to try to lean towards the notion of unity.

Humans are capable of sensing, feeling and thinking at the same time. It is important to know that at any moment all those aspects exist and attention to all three is necessary in order to be a wholly integrated person. We cannot, of course, be fully aware of all of them simultaneously. However, we can learn to flow between them in a rich and flexible way. The counsellor invites the client to have more awareness of all of themselves and to learn to move that awareness to the different aspects with easy and natural familiarity.

It is important to remember also that not everyone is stuck in the area of their thinking. Everybody has a preferred mode of experiencing. For some it is intellectual, for some emotional and for some physical. This leads to a preferred mode of expression and communication.

The counsellor notices that Jim reports on his thoughts to the exclusion of emotions and sensations. She gently invites him to focus on his body and notice what messages he is getting from his muscle tension, or what emotion he is feeling. Jill, who focuses chiefly on her bodily sensations — her headaches, the tensions in her body, the energy in her arms, and so on — may need help translating these emotions into feelings, naming them and thinking about them. Sally is mainly aware of her senses in relation to the outside world — what she is seeing or hearing around her. For her, the area of growth is to refer inward rather than outward. Equally, Sandra, who is strongly emotional, is asked by her counsellor to think about how she is understanding something: what sense she makes, what she thinks will happen, what she wants to do.

Facilitating Healthy 'Aggression'

Perls *et al* (1951) use the word 'aggression' to mean the proactive, self-fulfilling movement outwards towards the world and the environment. We all sometimes suppress this excitement for lots of reasons, some healthy, some not. We may quite properly hold back from running across the busy road to catch the bus, but we may unnecessarily hold back giving a compliment or making a complaint to a friend.

We have said that at the heart of Gestalt counselling is the relationship. It is in the relationship that counsellor and client make the contact through which a person experiences the excitement which, as long as it is unchecked, can lead to healthy 'aggressing' on the world. The counsellor's job is to help the client become aware of the way they make contact in the sessions and to allow that contact to become as vibrant as possible. The counsellor asks: Am I in contact with the client? What is the contact like? When does the client break the contact? How? What happens then? The counsellor reflects to the client what she has noticed so that he begins to be aware of what interruptions to contact or fixed gestalts are suppressing his natural excitement and his natural drive to reach out and 'agress' into the world.

Increasing Self-support

Self-support means the awareness of, and the ability to use, all internal and external resources and options. Put simply, it means doing whatever we need to do in order to feel confident enough to meet whatever situation arises in the best way we can. Perls *et al* (1951) say that self-support is to be fully in contact with the environment and the self — in a sense, the whole goal of Gestalt counselling.

A person who does not have self-support is likely to withdraw from their full experience of themselves in any moment of stress, reducing here-and-now contact and falling back on fixed gestalts. There are several ways to achieve self-support.

Physical Support

A self-supported person breathes evenly and at a depth which is both nourishing and comfortable. Their body posture is relaxed and evenly balanced so that their energy is contained and yet also accessible. They do not sit collapsed or crushed, they do not unsettle themselves by twisting limbs in awkward angles. Try an experiment yourself: sit on the edge of your chair and then slump back, relying on the chair back for support. Put your head on one side and lower your chin so that your breathing becomes more shallow. How do you feel? Now settle yourself comfortably on the seat with your weight evenly distributed. Straighten your head and relax your shoulders. Breathe deeply but comfortably. How do you feel now? It makes a surprising difference, doesn't it?

Contact Functions

Another important source of self-support is the ability and confidence to use all our contact functions. This can be done in many ways and will increase awareness. (Examples can be found in Chapter 4.) As the client is encouraged to focus on and trust their senses, they experience an enhanced excitement and a fuller quality of contact with themselves and the environment.

Being Present

Being fully self-supported includes being fully aware of what is happening in the present, having the ability to plan for the future and to keep our past experience available as a creative resource.

Using the Environment

People sometimes assume that being self-supported is the same as being self-sufficient. This is not necessarily true. It is not self-supporting to refuse help from the environment. Real self-support is having the ability honestly to use the environment for support when it is needed, yet trusting in the willingness and capability of others to help us. A self-supporting person knows the right time to call on the environment and the right person or persons to call upon: for instance, a driver calls the car breakdown service rather than leave themselves stranded on the motorway, or someone who has received shocking news goes to visit a friend.

Identifying with the Experience

Bob and Rita Resnick (1990, personal communication) say self-support is identifying with your experience. Under stress, we frequently retreat from our uncomfortable feelings precisely because they *are* uncomfortable or because they do not fit the image we have of ourselves. We distance ourselves from our anxiety while repressing part of our experience. Acknowledging and naming what is going on inside us can do much to free us, so that we can think about what we need and plan a way forward. This is true in traumatic situations such as bereavement, when we need to allow ourselves to recognize our feelings and responses, and it can also be true in more trivial situations such as feeling embarrassed if someone points out a mistake we have made.

Increasing Self-responsibility

The notion of self-responsibility is contained in the existential belief that we are fundamentally alone and we create our own meaning. Our task is to accept that we are fully responsible for our experience because we create and therefore in a sense choose it. Self-responsibility is a central principle of Gestalt counselling. As we become more aware of ourselves in our environment, we increase our knowledge and understanding of our needs and how we attempt to meet them as well as the ways in which we respond to people and events in our lives. We recognize that we choose our responses and that there are other ways in which we could choose to act, think or feel.

Here is an important implication for counselling. A client who has little self-awareness is unlikely to believe that they are responsible for their own experience. As they become more self-aware they become more capable of understanding how they create their own experience and can therefore start to feel more in charge of it. The considerate counsellor proceeds at the client's pace towards self-responsibility through growing awareness.

This process of increasing self-responsibility is in itself a powerful tool for change. John Harris, in his booklet, *Gestalt: an Idiosyncratic Introduction* (1989), presents a simple model of change based on three stages of increasing awareness and self-responsibility.

Stage One: 'This is how I am'

The first step towards change is to accept fully and without judgement the existence of all our feelings, thoughts and behaviour, even those which previously we have preferred not to notice. For instance, Alex complained that nobody liked her. In her counselling session, the counsellor invited her to look at her own behaviour. She realized that she treated her friends in a surly and critical way. At first she felt embarrassed about this but then, encouraged by her counsellor, she put aside her moral condemnation and 'owned' her surly behaviour. When we use the word 'owned' we do not mean 'owned up to', as in making a confession of a misdeed, we mean 'ownership'. She was able to say, "This behaviour is mine."

Stage Two: 'I am this way because I choose to be'

Having accepted ourselves as we are, the next stage is to recognize that, moment by moment, we are choosing how we respond to the world. At first this may seem hard, for often we feel as if we 'can't help it' or we say 'it' (or he or she or they) made me feel this way. Gradually, we begin to realize that there are other options. We may be acting according to choices made long ago that were creative adjustments at the time. The important question is how are we stopping ourselves making different choices in the present? Alex realized that, because she was expecting rebuffs from others, she approached them with suspicion and anger. At first it seemed impossible to her that she could choose to be different. How else could she respond? Her counsellor invited her to increase her awareness of how she made her meaning. She realized that she stopped herself welcoming her friends through fear of rejection. She protected herself by being the first to reject.

Stage Three: 'If I choose, I can be different'

In this stage of self-responsibility, we take control over our lives. We can choose to experiment with different ways of thinking and behaving. Sometimes this really can be as simple as it sounds. Sometimes the very act of becoming fully aware of who we are and how we keep ourselves that way can be enough for us to facilitate change in ourselves. Sometimes it can seem more difficult. It can involve taking a risk. After all, the familiar may be painful, but at least it is predictable. Newness involves the unexpected, which can be exciting but can also be frightening. However, we believe that, if we let ourselves become aware of our needs and wants, our natural drive for health and growth will emerge.

In our example, we left Alex beginning to recognize the possibility that she could respond differently to her friends. She began to see the many ways in which she could treat them warmly. First, she experimented with her counsellor, for, as you might expect, she had treated him with surliness and suspicion too. (Why would he be any different from others?) Letting herself be aware of her true feelings, she started to notice and comment on things that she liked about him. She shared the fact that she felt scared that he would not like her, and that she wanted him to like her. Then she tried behaving differently with people she met in the world, commenting on the things she liked instead of criticizing, asking them about themselves with interest and telling them about herself. Quite quickly she began to report that she was having very different relationships with her friends and family.

In the list of Gestalt principles we pointed out that a human being cannot exist apart from his environment. We are all part of a system of interaction and interdependence. Our example shows how a change in ourselves can have a marked impact on our environment. Taking responsibility for ourselves means also taking account of the consequences of our actions.

One last point about self-responsibility. We are implying here that we have total choice about how we are in the world. Of course, this is not always the case. It would be rather pointless to discuss whether or not we *can* be 'made' to feel something if we are defenceless children, for instance, or if we are starving or being tortured. However, while we cannot be responsible for everything that happens to us, we can be one hundred per cent responsible for our reactions and the meaning we make. Social deprivation or psychological abuse can make it hard for us to feel as if we have any choice in our responses. Nevertheless, even in extreme circumstances people have been known to show astonishing and moving strength in continuing to be responsible for how they feel, think and behave. Examples of this kind are described most beautifully in *Man's Search for Meaning*, by Victor Frankl (1964), which concerns experiences in a concentration camp; in Bruno Bettelheim's *The Informed Heart* (1986), which treats the same subject; and more recently in Brian Keenan's account of his years as a hostage, *An Evil Cradling* (1992).

Educating

●

There is a sense in which Gestalt counsellors are educating their clients from the moment they arrive with us. We may ask them how they feel about being here, we may remark on their sighing, or the fact that they hesitated before mentioning their family, and so on. We are educating them to pay attention to themselves and to become aware of who they are. However, there are occasions when a counsellor may educate by actually giving information.

Normally a Gestalt counsellor does not teach a client. This would imply imposing one's own values on the client, which would go completely against Gestalt philosophy. While it would be impossible to pretend that we can totally put aside our beliefs and values, we as counsellors do our best to bracket them. At the very least we are alert to our own prejudices. However, there are times when it can be appropriate and useful to 'teach' a client — when we believe that they lack information about something. It may be non-directive to allow a person to struggle with a problem when we know that there is important information which may help to solve it, but in our opinion it may sometimes be disrespectful and even unethical not to share solutions.

Ruth was complaining about how tense and agitated she always seemed to be. She said that she was "in a constant state of mild anxiety. I don't know why." Later, she revealed that she was a 'coffee freak' and normally drank at least one or two cups an hour at work. The counsellor checked whether Ruth knew about the stimulating effects of caffeine and she did not. She decided to give up caffeine for a while, and the counsellor warned her that she was likely to get a headache for a day or so as a withdrawal reaction.

It can be helpful to clients to give them a brief explanation of healthy process as we see it, telling them about contact and interruptions, about unfinished business or self-responsibility. There are several reasons for doing this. The first is that many people enjoy and benefit from being given the theoretical model so that they can apply it to themselves. Clients often find that this sort of information helps them to feel competent and hopeful. There is also an argument for saying that it is actually more ethical for a counsellor to share their frame of reference. Instead of its being an unspoken influence on the client, it is clearly offered as an approach and the client is free to take or leave it as they choose.

Another example of counsellor educating client is found in the area of relationships. Many people lack information about social skills: safer sex, self-expression — what Steiner (1984) called 'emotional literacy' — and so on. It can be helpful if the counsellor is able to address the deficits in the client's education. This may involve referring a client to an appropriate agency or self-help group.

The rule of thumb in this area, as in all counselling, is that educating needs to take place within the framework created by the phenomenological method, the dialogue and the field, so that the counsellor is responding to a clear gestalt of the client's emerging need in the context of their life.

To summarize, however much we hope to meet our client in a spirit of open-mindedness, having bracketed our own prejudices, it is impossible to pretend that we do not have certain values about health. It seems logical that, as counsellors, committed to the health and growth of our clients, we work to promote this vision of health. We have offered five areas which we believe to be central to the Gestalt approach to healthy process.

Exercises

1(a)   What is your major channel of expression — feeling, thinking or sensing? Make a point of practising referring to all your functions regularly so that you expand your experience of yourself. You may find that you are most comfortable taking them in a particular order. Some people prefer thinking, then feeling, then sensing; some feeling, thinking, sensing; and so on. Experiment with them all and see if you can find your preferred path.

(b) Start to notice the preferred channels of your clients and respectfully invite them to extend their awareness of themselves.

2(a) Go through the list of methods of self-support. Let yourself be aware of which of these are areas of strength for you. What can you do about the other areas?

(b) With clients, notice the moment when they lose self-support. One way you may see it is in the way they interrupt contact with you. Explore with them how they have done this. It may be that they have lost touch with themselves or are repressing some feeling of discomfort. It may be that they are interrupting through projection or retroflection and so on. Explore the interruption and invite your client to think about what methods of self-support have worked for them in the past and whether they could be used again. Offer support as they regain their balance and make contact with you once more.

3 Think of an incident that you felt annoyed about. Recount it to a partner in a way which takes no responsibility for it. For example: the car was going along the High Street and suddenly there was a woman crossing the road in front of me. The car swerved and nearly hit a lamp-post. It was really awful. The car just missed it and nearly went out of control. And when the journey was over, it seemed that the eggs had fallen on the floor of the car and been broken. It was so annoying.

Tell the story again, this time using the language of self-responsibility. For example: I was driving the car along the High Street. I was thinking of something else and suddenly I realized that a woman had started to cross the road in front of me. I swerved to avoid her and drove straight towards a lamp-post. I was really scared. I pulled the steering wheel round, swerved again and for a moment thought I was losing control of the car. When I had finished my journey, I noticed that, when I had swerved, I had dislodged the eggs onto the floor of the car and broken them. I was really annoyed.

You will notice the profound difference in the two ways of telling the story.

Chapter 12

BUILDING AN EXPERIMENT

What is an Experiment?

When clients are experiencing difficulties in their lives, it is likely that they are limited in options: restricted in their ways of thinking, feeling and behaving. One of the techniques that a counsellor may use to help a client expand their options is to offer a procedure usually referred to as an experiment. An experiment is an experience at a critical point in the counselling session where action seems appropriate to assist the client. It is usually designed by the counsellor but sometimes by the client. Experiments use imagination and enactment to expand the experience of the client in order to heighten awareness, clarify an emerging figure, intensify feeling or literally experiment with new ways of being and behaving.

The aim of an experiment is to challenge the client's habitual patterns and to offer alternatives. Mackewn (1994) says, 'the client tries out new behaviours, and *sees what happens*' (emphasis in original). Like any new experience, this can often feel frightening or strange, so while they may sometimes take place outside the consulting room (as 'homework') it is often preferable that such experiential learning happens first in the safe container of the counselling situation. Perls *et al* (1951) called this contained procedure the 'safe emergency'. It is an interesting use of the word 'emergency' to imply both danger and the emerging figure.

Zinker (1977) writes, 'Most experiments have one quality in common — they ask the client to express something behaviourally, rather than to merely cognize or experience internally.' For example, Christina, in a flat and formal way, tells her group about the successful completion of a difficult and challenging piece of work. When she is asked if she wants anything from the group, she says, again in rather a prim way, that she would like people to acknowledge how well she has done. The counsellor notices that, as she is talking, Christina has her arms firmly folded across her chest. She invites Christina to stand up, hold her arms out and shout, "I've finished my work. I did it wonderfully!" Christina does so and the group sees her come alive as she 'owns' her excitement and pleasure in herself.

Charles is recounting a story about how badly he has been treated by his car mechanic. The counsellor observes that, as he complains, he is jiggling his foot. She invites him to become aware of his foot and to exaggerate the movement. As he does so, he begins a kicking movement and very quickly connects with his retroflected anger. This he releases by kicking a cushion around the room. He sits down feeling lighter.

The Stages of an Experiment

●

The building of an experiment follows certain steps. They are not followed rigidly: the counsellor and client move through them fluidly, shuttling between them as the process unfolds. We have chosen to use the stages of the cycle of experience to illustrate them. A summary appears in Table 1.

Step One: Sensation

In this stage the counsellor's task is to be in a dialogue with her client, using the phenomenological method to observe and remark on the content, the process and the field of the client. She remains as open as possible, intervening only to meet the client, with empathy, to heighten awareness and sharpen the figures.

Step Two: Recognition

The task of the counsellor and client in this stage is to recognize the theme or themes which start to unfold. The counsellor observes the figure or figures emerging from the ground of the client's thoughts, feelings and behaviour. Sometimes one figure carries a greater charge of energy than the others and this may be what attracts the counsellor to focus on this theme for the experiment. At other times there may be several equally charged figures, between which the counsellor identifies a unifying theme on which to base the experiment. There may also be times when the emerging figure for the counsellor is an area which seems vital but is being ignored, and they decide to make this the focus of the experiment.

Stage	Counsellor's task and focus
Sensation	Noticing the emerging theme
Recognition	Recognition and sharpening of the emerging theme
Appraisal/planning	Attention to timing Choice of the level of risk Choice of format/procedure Negotiation, adaptation and acceptance
Action	Initial execution and adaptations
Contact	Full contact with the experience
Assimilation/completion	Completion of the experience Integration and making sense
Withdrawal	Withdrawal of energy and interest

Table 1 *Stages of an experiment*

The theme for an experiment does not rely solely on content but on the juxtaposition of content, process and the emerging figures. Bob, for example, is talking a great deal about his mother. Now and again he refers to her cruel criticism. As he does so, he has his eyes lowered to the floor, rarely looking at the counsellor. With this information at her disposal, as well as the knowledge she has from previous sessions of Bob's low sense of self-worth and his sexual abuse, the counsellor is deciding which theme to follow. The possible themes could include exploring Bob's introjection of his verbally and physically abusing mother; his projection of his mother onto others; his self-criticism; his low self-worth and his lack of eye contact. She is aware that criticism is a thread which runs through the figures. Also it seems to be currently carrying most energy for Bob. She waits to allow other shifts of energy which may validate her observation.

In these last few paragraphs we have been describing, from the counsellor's viewpoint, some of what she might do. This may give the impression that the direction of the session is in the total power of the counsellor. This is not the case. As Mackewn (1994) says, 'Gestalt counselling is a co-created experience.' It 'is experimental from moment to moment, in the sense that neither counsellor nor client can predict the unfolding process of the session'.

Step Three: Appraisal and Planning

TIMING

The timing of experiments is important within the context of a single session and within the developing relationship with the counsellor over time. In some of the videos of Fritz Perls' work, he moves into experiments with his clients within minutes of meeting them. This is sometimes a powerful and expedient form of intervention. On the other hand, in its very speed it may undermine the trust between client and counsellor or may focus attention on something that was just a 'warming-up' to the more important issue for the client. For example, inviting Steve to experiment with completing the sentence, "I want to miss . . ." when he arrives five minutes late for a session may be irrelevant or even abusive if this is his first time of being late, whereas it may be a potent intervention if he has a history of arriving late.

Sometimes what marks the difference between an effective and a less effective counsellor is not so much the creativity of the experiment as this very matter of timing. The less effective counsellor often pounces upon the first opportunity for an experiment and pre-empts the client's process or delays the intervention until the moment is past and the client feels drawn back into something which is no longer foreground. For the effective practitioner, good timing means respecting the client's unfolding process, of which the experiment itself becomes a part rather than a distraction.

If in doubt, wait. By waiting you can give yourself the opportunity to question yourself as to whether your investment in the experiment at that moment is more for your needs than the client's. Sometimes a counsellor may be especially invested in an experiment because of their need to 'do something helpful' or even because, without awareness, they sense a need to do the experiment for themselves. By waiting you can also gather more information from the client which will validate or invalidate your ideas.

Certain experiments will depend upon foundations that must be laid by other experiments. Their timing, therefore, may be developmentally determined. Bob, for example, had identified several themes concerning his sexuality as a teenager. The counsellor had some ideas for experiments with the 'sixteen-year-old Bob' who seemed to be emerging, but saved them for some appropriate future session, deciding that Bob's much younger and repeated experiences of sexual abuse would need to be worked with before he could safely use any therapeutic experiments concerning sexuality.

FOCUS AND LEVEL OF EXPERIMENTS

The level of a therapeutic experiment will depend upon the client, the counsellor and the setting in which they practise. It will take into account the readiness of the client, their self-support and their present circumstances outside the sessions. Some experiments are deep and/or complex. They move to areas which may have been out of the client's awareness for many years, challenging core beliefs and ways of being. These experiments are appropriate for clients who have already established a trusting alliance with their counsellor over a period of time. Despite this connection there may be occasions when the use of deep experiments is not appropriate, even with a very experienced client, for instance during a time of difficult life circumstances.

Furthermore, if deep or complex experiments are used within a single session, ensure that enough time is allowed for their integration before the client leaves the safety of the consulting room. For example, when working with Bob at a time when his wife is seriously ill in hospital, the counsellor avoids pitching experiments at a level which could leave Bob more fragile than usual and in greater need of support from those close to him.

The grading of experiments will involve consideration of various aspects of the counselling situation. The counsellor will take into account the level of *intimacy* appropriate to the situation. For example, asking Bob to make eye contact with her would require a higher level of intimacy than asking him to notice where he is looking. Another element which can be graded is that of *perceived risk*. An experiment will often cause a client to feel some degree of fear as they try something new. This is very natural, and of course fear is very akin to excitement. However, the level of fear should not be too high or it will cause more stress than benefit. It is advisable for counsellor and client to think about what might be a small risk initially and then expand it by degrees. If you find that a client, having agreed to an experiment, 'hits some resistance', it may be that the experiment has been pitched too high in riskiness and a less challenging idea can be found. It may be also that the experiment is too confrontational to a person's core beliefs about themselves and further exploration is needed. This will be discussed further later on.

A client's preferred *mode of functioning* (that is feeling, thinking or sensing) may be a relevant factor. Unless the purpose of the experiment is actually to extend or integrate these functions, it may be useful to choose one which uses the client's 'strong suit' while they take the risk of pushing the boundaries in a less familiar area. Thus Susan, who was easily in touch with her feelings but did not readily think about them and what they meant, was invited first to express her anger in an unstructured way to her father whom she imagined on the chair opposite her. Then she used her thinking to put into words what it was she was angry about and what she wanted.

The counsellor will also design the *structure* of an experiment, taking heed of the particular circumstances relevant to the situation. Sometimes a simple structure can have a profound impact, such as when Jake, who had a severe burn on his hand, was asked to imagine himself as that hand and then to talk as if he were his hand.

The counsellor will need to think about the physical *space* for an experiment. The area used may range from the client's chair as she sits quietly thinking about something, to the client moving about the room or, on some occasions, leaving the consulting room altogether. It may be appropriate, for example, to go for a walk to the park or to the shops. It may even be desirable to meet the client at a preplanned special place, such as a building with a lift, so as to work on the client's fear of enclosed spaces. The *time continuum* is another factor affecting the grading of an experiment. In Gestalt, all time frames are possible. Sometimes it is assumed that, as the essence of Gestalt is working in the 'here and now', this precludes using the 'there and then' of our past and future. However, this is not so. Clients can do work to change their present lives using experiments that range from them working as if they are the embryo they once were, through any developmental stage of their lives, right through to their anticipated death. The essential feature of the experiment is that it is imagined and enacted in the present *as the present* — what is called the 'then and now'.

CHOOSING FORMATS AND PROCEDURES FOR EXPERIMENTS

There are innumerable formats for experiments which include self-sensitization, role-play and enactment, empty-chair work, guided fantasy, creative expression using various media, dreamwork, encounter with another or others and experiments for the client to do between sessions.

Self-sensitization.   This type of experiment involves any suggestion given to the client aimed at increasing their awareness of their body, posture, tone, gesture, attire or tensions. An example here is inviting Muriel to exaggerate the stroking of her top lip with her thumb.

Role-play and enactment.   In this type of experiment the counsellor may invite the client to act out different aspects of themselves, how they might be in particular situations or even other personae, such as those of other people, animals or even things which are currently of significance in the client's real or fantasy life. For example, Peter is invited to become the dinosaur in the dream he has just reported.

Empty-chair work.   Here the client is invited to address an imagined other (again this could be an aspect of themselves, another person, animal, quality or thing) in a space usually opposite them and often represented by an empty chair or cushion. Beatrice, for example, is invited to imagine her depression in the empty chair and to begin a dialogue with that externalized part of her.

Guided fantasy.   This is a form of experiment where the clients are invited to be physically passive and relaxed while the counsellor uses techniques offering the clients opportunities to use their creative imagination to expand and explore their options for managing their present circumstances. It is important that the counsellor uses 'open phrases' and generalized concepts in setting the scene so that it is the client's symbols and images which are developed — not the counsellor's. John is extremely tense and nervous about his forthcoming driving test. He requests a guided fantasy from the counsellor which will assist him in being relaxed and successful. His counsellor asks him to find a relaxed position in the counselling room. She chooses a tape of soothing and unobtrusive music which helps John to move away from the overstructured left hemisphere of his brain, and connect with his more creative right hemisphere. She then suggests that he find a time in his life when he had achieved something he wanted and was feeling good. She takes time to guide him through the details of the scene as though it were happening in the present. She alerts his awareness to all his senses, asking him to notice what he can see, smell, hear and feel, how his body is positioned, who else is there, and so on. She particularly invites him to focus on whatever he is feeling at that moment of triumph. Then, as a way of linking this past success to his future ambition, she invites him to choose, in his imagination, something from the scene, a totem or talisman, which he can bring back as a support for himself. She next asks him to project himself forward to the time of his driving test, to allow himself to imagine having his chosen totem in the car with him and to vividly imagine a successful test. She closes by reminding him that he will be relaxed yet alert on stopping the fantasy. She then instructs him to come out of the fantasy and be fully aware of the present moment, making contact with her and the room around him.

The example illustrates the use of various hypnotic induction techniques such as relaxation, the use of unusual juxtapositions of images, the lulling of the left brain and the invitation to the imagination of the right. And so on. It is important to remember that some people respond very powerfully to these techniques. Do not use this type of fantasy with someone that you do not know well unless you are sure that their usual grasp on reality is very strong. Someone who finds life disorienting already will not be helped by such an experience. Also pay careful attention to safety procedures. It is useful to say at an early stage, "If I use an image which is not useful or relevant to you, simply ignore it." At the end, you must give as much attention to the 'coming out' of the fantasy as to the going in, naming all the stages of return-ing to the here and now.

Creative expression using various media.   There is almost no limit to what can be used to assist in an experiment. Some of the more common are pens, pencils, crayons, paints, clay, sticky paper, mud, beads, soft toys, plants, kitchen utensils, food, old maga-zines, baby equipment, water and sand. We invite you to add to the list. Some counsellors choose to use a variety of different materials to assist with their experiments. Others tend to make their experiments part of the dialogue and do not use 'props'. There is no right or wrong about this; what is important is for you to use whatever blends well with your personal style and is appropriate for your clients. If you do wish to have equipment available for experiments, you may wish to think about whether you keep it out of sight, for instance in a cupboard; in that way, it is part of the counsellor's field but not that of the client, so that the client's process is not artificially distracted. On the other hand, you may want to have it in full view in order to stimulate clients into initiating their own experiments.

Jean cannot connect with a childhood experience, remaining detached and 'grown-up' as she talks about a very important time when she had not felt in control of her life. The counsellor gives her paper and pencils and suggests she write her name in childish handwriting, using her non-dominant left hand, not her dominant right hand. Jean at first giggles as she wrestles with the task, and then spontaneously connects with the unexpressed feelings from that incident in her childhood.

Dreamwork. 'Perls saw the dream as an added bonus in the form of an existential message which tells us exactly where we are in relation to ourselves and to the world at the present time. Whereas Freud called the dream the "royal road to the unconscious", Perls called it the "royal road to integration" because he saw in it the possibility of reclaiming the lost parts of the personality and becoming whole' (Ann Faraday, 1973). Many Gestalt practitioners hold the belief that all aspects of a dream are projections of some aspect of the dreamer themselves. We think that there are five different types of dreams: (1) dreams connected with everyday issues in the present; this type of dream may evoke problem solving, attention focusing, practising and confirming salient skills and successes, and discharging unexpressed feelings; (2) resolving the past in the present; here a dream may help by providing missing developmental links, integrating traumatic experiences or 'owning' disowned aspects of oneself; (3) preparing for the future; (4) communal or shared dreams; and (5) spiritual and supernatural dreams (see Fish and Lapworth, 1994).

> Perls . . . perceived each aspect of the dream as a part of the dreamer's personality. Thus, working with the dream involves re-owning and reclaiming those parts of the dreamer which have been projected away from themselves onto characters and objects contained within their dream-story. In this way, a dreamer dreaming of a car journey might usefully explore being the car, the road, the destination, the scenery, the speed and so on. Perls would ask someone wishing to report a dream to recount it in the present tense. This was to re-experience some of the original vitality and intensity as well as to take ownership of its various components making it truly relevant to the dreamer's present life situation. For example, 'I am driving from London to Glasgow. I am in a blue car. I cannot find the main road but I cannot stop. I am tired. I now see a road sign' and so on. Having recounted the whole dream in the present tense, the dreamer then recounts the dream from the

point of view of various aspects of the dream — 'I am a blue car. I am being driven by a scatter-brained young woman who is trying to take me to Scotland.' In this example, when the dreamer mentioned being 'blue', she began to cry as she realised she was depressed and the way she stopped herself knowing this was to 'drive' herself incessantly to work hard and to keep going. (Fish and Lapworth, 1994)

NEGOTIATION, ADAPTATION AND ACCEPTANCE OF THE EXPERIMENT

Having decided that it is a suitable moment for a certain experiment, the counsellor needs to introduce it to the client. Sometimes it will be appropriate simply to suggest that the client do something. Jean has just been reliving a dream from the perspective of the main image in it, that of a colourful kite. She has just said, "Someone keeps tugging my string" and the counsellor tells her, "Say that again." We are using the word experiment to include all the interventions which, by heightening awareness, invite the client into new areas of experiencing. These do not need negotiating and are part of the relationship between counsellor and client.

At other times it is important to offer an experiment to a client and gain their agreement. Deborah has been working on her inability to stand by her own opinions in the face of loud opposition. Remembering some details of her family of origin, the counsellor asks Deborah if she would be willing to do an experiment around a family meal. Deborah asks for more details and the counsellor tells how she remembers that Deborah was the youngest in the family and was often bullied by her siblings and overbearing father. She suggests that Deborah have (role-play) a family meal and choose others in the counselling group to represent the members of her original family. The counsellor suggests that at some time during the meal Deborah may find some way of facing her oppressors. Deborah thinks about this and then agrees, saying that Sunday lunch would be the most appropriate meal for the experiment.

Another example of negotiation involves Felicity, who is offered an experiment of tearing up a newspaper to undo some of her retroflected anger. She agrees that a tearing action is exactly what she needs but that newspaper is too messy as the print comes off on her hands. An old magazine is chosen instead.

Step Four: Action

As the client puts the experiment into its initial execution, further adaptions of the experiment may be necessary. Once an experiment has begun it is important that the counsellor monitors and adjusts it as necessary so that it continues to be of benefit to the client. While talking to her husband in the empty chair opposite her, Margaret becomes very angry and starts slapping her own thigh. The counsellor quickly intervenes to stop this potentially hurtful retroflection. She asks Margaret to make some other gesture to express her anger.

Step Five: Contact

The stage of full contact is usually a short one. It belongs entirely to the client as they immerse themselves completely in the experience. They need no further guidance from the counsellor, who keeps out of the way of the process. This may be the moment of full expression or realization of meaning. In the example given above, after Jean repeats, "Someone keeps tugging my string", the counsellor waits with her as Jean lets herself experience the implication of what she is saying. She begins to sob out her realization that she is still responding to the restrictions imposed by her mother.

Step Six: Assimilation and Completion

Once an experiment is completed, time is needed for the client to make sense of their new experience and integrate it. The amount of time required may vary from seconds to minutes or longer.

After tearing up the old magazine, Felicity flops back, breathing heavily. She looks at the pile of paper in front of her for a few minutes and then, laughing, gathers up bits of it and tosses them into the air. During Deborah's Sunday lunch, she eventually stands on the table and tells her bossy brothers to shut up. This gives her immediate relief and pleasure. During the assimilation and completion phase, she shares with the other group members how different she felt during the experiment and thinks about other situations in which she can, and will, be more assertive.

Step Seven: Withdrawal

At this stage the client withdraws energy from the experiment and allows it to fade into the ground of his awareness. At this time, it is probably important not to talk a lot about the experiment or divert energy too quickly back into some aspect of it. For the moment the client is at rest before a new sensation arises. Often, during this withdrawal, the client continues to make sense of his experience. The effects of it may emerge gradually in the ensuing days or weeks.

Fuller Examples of Experiments

In the following examples the transcripts of the counselling work are annotated in a different typeface to indicate the stages of the experiment. In the first example, the experiment flows naturally without the need for negotiation or grading. The counsellor simply offers a suggestion to which the client responds.

Simon

Simon is talking about preparations for his final examination.

sensation and recognition of an emerging figure

SIMON: Several of my friends are taking the exam in July. I know I could too. I want to take it. My trainers and supervisor say I'm ready, but somehow I'm too scared. Maybe I'm not really ready. I just don't know what's best to do. This has happened to me before. Whenever I have to face some big test I get really anxious and don't know what to do.

COUNSELLOR: So this seems to be a pattern for you, that when you are under stress you get tense and anxious and don't know what to do.

SIMON: Yes, absolutely.

COUNSELLOR: I'm aware that your breathing is very shallow and that your body seems tense and constricted.

SIMON: Yes I feel like a piano wire ready to snap.

appraisal and planning
sharpening the figure

COUNSELLOR: I suggest you stay with your awareness and see if you can really feel the tension in your body.

SIMON: OK, it feels like it's getting stronger as I'm more aware of it, it's like . . . I really want to do something, I've got all this energy . . .

offering the experiment

COUNSELLOR: And as you say that, you are sitting completely still. I have a suggestion, if you're interested.

SIMON: Yes, what?

COUNSELLOR: Get up out of your seat and start to walk up and down.

action

(*Simon starts pacing up and down briskly*)

COUNSELLOR: How do you feel now?

SIMON: I feel stronger somehow, as if I am more in control.

COUNSELLOR: OK. Keep moving, and tell me what you are thinking now.

SIMON: That I don't want this exam to lick me, that I want to be in control.

COUNSELLOR: Your voice sounds strong and convincing as you say that. "I want to be in control."

SIMON: Does it?

COUNSELLOR: Yes. You sound surprised.

SIMON: I don't see myself as strong or in control.

COUNSELLOR: How come?

SIMON: I always thought my father knew best when I was a child and I was never allowed to argue with him. He was always in control.

COUNSELLOR: Was he in control about exams?

SIMON: Oh yes. I remember, when I was taking my 'O' levels, he told me I had to get better grades than my brother. That scared me as I wasn't very good at some of the subjects and I felt this enormous pressure to try and do better than I thought I was capable of. I got more and more scared and I couldn't seem to get on with my work.

COUNSELLOR: What would you want to say to your father if you could go back and speak to him?

contact

SIMON: (*stops pacing and clenches his fists*) Leave me alone. Let me do the exams my way. I can only do my best. (*looks at counsellor*) Yes, I really wanted to say that to him. I can picture his face now. He wouldn't like to hear that, but I don't care.

COUNSELLOR: How are you feeling now you've said that?

assimilation and completion

SIMON: I feel much clearer. I don't feel so tense. And I've just realized something. The reason I'm so anxious about this exam is that my friends are taking it and I feel as if I've got to compete against them to see if I can do better than them.

COUNSELLOR: Is that really important to you?

SIMON: I can see now that I don't need to; it doesn't matter who is better. I want to just do my best — for me . . . (*pauses*) I feel so much better now. A weight has been lifted off my shoulders. I could almost see me enjoying taking the exam!

COUNSELLOR: You look pleased and excited now.

SIMON: Yes. I will take that exam in July.

withdrawal

COUNSELLOR: Is there anything more you need about that now?

SIMON: No. I feel finished.

Molly

In the following example, the experiment is graded and negotiated at the appraisal stage.

sensation and recognition of theme

MOLLY: I'm going to South America for a holiday and want to do something about my enormous fear of cockroaches before I go. Maybe I'll see lots there and I'm worried that I'll lose control.

appraisal, planning and negotiation

COUNSELLOR: I'm hearing you have two fears — one of cockroaches and another of losing control.

MOLLY: Yes, I suppose that I do but the second one is only likely to happen if I see a cockroach.

COUNSELLOR: Do you want to face your fear here with me?

MOLLY: I suppose so.

COUNSELLOR: You don't sound very sure.

MOLLY: Well, I am scared but . . . Yes, I really do want to do something about this.

COUNSELLOR: OK. I'd like to suggest something; tell me how this sounds to you. Imagine there's a cockroach on the floor in front of you.

MOLLY: Uurh — no — I couldn't. That's much too scary.

COUNSELLOR: How scary on a scale of one to ten?

MOLLY: About seven.

COUNSELLOR: How scary would it be to draw one on the whiteboard?

MOLLY: About a three or four.

COUNSELLOR: Are you willing to try that with that level of scare?

MOLLY: Yes, I'll try, but even thinking about its shape makes me feel like shaking.

COUNSELLOR: I suggest you draw it while letting yourself shake as much as you want to.

action

MOLLY: (*at the board*) They have long black bodies like this and large, raspy legs and wings . . . ugh . . . I can't go on . . . this is horrible. (*She drops the pen and starts winding her hands into the hem of her jersey*)

COUNSELLOR: You look very small and helpless right now.

MOLLY: (*nods and after a while uses a tiny voice*) I don't want to see it . . . I don't want to touch it.

COUNSELLOR: (*moving next to Molly*) Where is it Molly?

contact

MOLLY: He's going to put it in my hair. (*Molly bursts into tears and covers her head with her hands*) Make him take it away.

COUNSELLOR: I'm here Molly, I'm with you.

MOLLY: (*cries deeply, then turns to counsellor*) What shall I do?

COUNSELLOR: Tell him to stop.

MOLLY: Stop it. Stop it. STOP IT . . . (*pauses*) . . . I didn't stop him then, but I would damn well stop him now! (*Molly stops and looks thoughtful*)

assimilation and completion

COUNSELLOR: What's happening now Molly?

MOLLY: I feel relieved. I'm thinking about that time. My brother used to tease and torment me awfully. One day he threatened to put a big, black beetle in my hair. I can still see its legs wriggling as he held it over my face. I think I wet myself in terror and I was terribly ashamed of my wet pants and dress.

COUNSELLOR: What do you think the beetle would have done if your brother hadn't been holding it?

MOLLY: I expect it was as frightened as I was and would have run away if it could.

COUNSELLOR: What do you suppose cockroaches in South America might do if you meet them there?

MOLLY: Hopefully, skedaddle.

COUNSELLOR: What's the worst that would happen if they don't?

MOLLY: Well, if the worst is me wetting my pants I suppose I'd survive that. If I see there are loads of them there I could carry an extra pair in my handbag. (*laughs*)

COUNSELLOR: You surely could, or an anti-insect spray of some sort!

MOLLY: I wish there had been an ally like you back then.

COUNSELLOR: Would you complete your picture on the board in some way Molly, so that you end this work in a way that suits you?

MOLLY: Yes. (*She finishes the diagram of the cockroach and then adds a stickperson attacking it with an enormous repellent. She adds a face of comic terror to the cockroach and an expression of triumph to the person's face*)

COUNSELLOR: (*laughs*) That's terrific. You're terrific.

withdrawal

Exercises

●

We suggest that you try these exercises now, in order to get in touch with your own creativity, and then practise them again after you have read the next chapter, 'The Experimental Environment'. By definition, the ideas for experiments emerge in the moment, as the individual experiences direction of their energy, how they may be blocking, and what release they need. It is difficult, therefore, to suggest exercises in creating experiments. However, here are a few suggestions for you to play with.

Practise thinking about the timing and content of experiments by watching characters on the television. If you have access to a video machine, so much the better. Watch a film or play and let yourself notice when a person is blocking their healthy process with an interruption to contact, a fixed gestalt, and so on. Halt the film on 'Pause' and take your time to imagine what experiments you would design for that person.

Enlist the support of a fellow trainee and take it in turns to talk and listen. Identify moments of high energy. Then discuss what experiment may be suitable. As you become more confident, allow your hunches and intuition to come to the fore. Remember to practise the phenomenological method, so that you will be open to a wide range of options as you flow with the emerging figures.

Lastly, try two experiments with your own boundaries and options.

What is going on inside you now? Did you answer with a feeling, a thought, a sensation or an action? Experiment with giving answers with the other three.

You are now finishing this chapter. Let yourself know what would be a typical thing for you to do now. Experiment with doing something very different!

Chapter 13

THE EXPERIMENTAL ENVIRONMENT

In this chapter we talk about some of the situations in which a counsellor might suggest an experiment. The function of experiments in Gestalt counselling is to offer new potential figures to the client. They emerge from the process of the session, and neither counsellor nor client should constrain themselves by becoming attached to a particular desired outcome. The experiment should be an adventure of discovery.

Having said that, there are times when experiments will address specific areas in which change may be desired by the client and so inevitably take on a focus or aim. It is important that the counsellor remain steadfast in her attitude that the experiment is to explore options — not to find the 'right way'. The experiment is offered with respect and flexibility to a person who may be stuck with no creative resources at that moment. In this sense, it is an energizer which may mobilize the client to follow their own direction — sometimes to a completely unexpected outcome.

For the sake of simplicity we have categorized experiments into three general, major areas: (1) heightening awareness, (2) restoring healthy self-regulation and (3) exploring and developing new behaviour and skills. Many areas, of course, are not discrete and there is much overlapping and interweaving. However, we will look at each category separately, offering some examples of experiments in each. We invite you to notice how one may lead to another. When you are counselling, invent your own experiments — ones which occur to you naturally as the session unfolds. Experiments which *emerge from* the dialogue are the ones which have most value. As Yontef (1991) says, 'The combining of dialogue and phenomenological experimentation is one of the valuable and unique contributions of Gestalt therapy.'

You will notice that some of the interventions in this part of the book have been described elsewhere. Many of the routes for heightening awareness or restoring self-regulation would arise automatically out of the phenomenological method. In that case, of course, the stages of building an experiment described in Chapter 12 would not be necessary as the interventions are a natural part of your dialogue with the client. However, we include them here as we believe that any intervention on the part of the counsellor which has the effect of changing the client's direction is, in a sense, inviting them to experiment.

Heightening Awareness
●

Sharpening the Figure

Much of what the counsellor does in terms of interventions will fall into the category of sharpening the figure. For this reason, we are looking at this type of experiment in some detail. The aim for the client is to have as full an experience of her thoughts, feelings and actions as possible. This can be facilitated in a number of ways. The counsellor chooses to focus on aspects of the client and her story, in detail, aware that anything and everything may be relevant. Thus comments like "You sighed as you said that", "Notice what your hand is doing", "What does that word mean to you?", "What sense are you making of that?" or "Where in your body are you feeling that?", and so on, are all ways of sharpening the figure.

Polster (1987, 1991) talks about what he calls 'psychological slippage', by which he means a looseness of direction, an unconnectedness of ideas in a client's discourse. He offers a method of 'tightening the sequences' whereby the counsellor aims to guide the client to 'follow the natural directions of his words and actions, one after another, with a minimum of circumlocution, qualification, allusion, illogicality, self-suppression'. The client can then be swept into a stream of 'continuing nextness', the natural flow of which both limits the sense of fear because of its 'rightness' and enhances the vibrancy of the figure. Thus the client accentuates what may be veiled and connects their experience to natural consequences. For example, if you are dimly aware that you are sad, you may do nothing but complain. But if you become fully aware of your feeling you may connect it to its natural expression, crying, or to a memory or to a desire or a decision. And so on.

Polster offers us three dimensions which are relevant to tight sequences. The first is the difference between real contact and transference (the replaying of a past relationship in the present). Tight sequencing means that either one or the other should be done fully — not, as usually happens, a mixture of both. So the counsellor may help the client to 'unhook' the transference, for instance by suggesting direct eye contact, or she may invite the client to go more fully into the transference projection by making the connection with a memory of a father or mother.

The second dimension is the relationship between awareness and action. Awareness on its own, says Polster, leads to compacted energy, 'implosiveness' or dreaminess. Equally, action without awareness is mechanical, purposeless and unrewarding. A counsellor helps a client to make a connection between what he is aware of and the actions which might accompany that. Thus it could be the awareness of a feeling and its expression, as in the example of sadness above. Alternatively, the counsellor could invite the client to link what they are talking about to an apparently incongruent or unconnected action.

For example, Joan is talking about a difficulty with her husband, who is often wanting to have sex when she would rather not. Her voice is quite calm and reasonable as she explores the issue, taking great care to see it from both sides. The counsellor notices that she is continuously brushing her skirt as she speaks and asks the woman to exaggerate it very slightly. Immediately, she becomes aware of a feeling of anger as she firmly brushes something away from her. Raising her voice she says, "Get off me!" and uses both hands to brush her skirt with a pushing motion. This action stimulates another thread of awareness as she remembers being trapped and molested by a group of boys at her school. Her anger turns to rage as she verbally and physically defends herself in a way she could not do at the time.

The example shows how cognitive awareness became linked, first, to unaware action, then to aware action, which led to a deeper awareness, and so on. Later in this chapter you will find many experiments which aim to tighten the connection between awareness and action.

The third dimension is the relationship between abstraction and detail. Basically, abstracting means the generalizing of details into a summarizing statement. Detailing means describing the specific elements of an experience, situation or event. Polster makes the analogy of the difference between a chapter and its title. He stresses that we cannot do counselling with just titles. Using generalizations, a client and counsellor may discuss something together on an abstract basis, 'settling for ... empty and distorted understandings' and making assumptions that they each know what the other means. Inviting a client to be specific — saying, for instance, to John: "You say your dad comes and shits on you. What exactly does that mean, how does he shit on you?" — invites him away from complaining in an 'Isn't it awful' way into telling *his true story*, the one that happened to *him*, the one which carries his real feelings and thoughts. If you wish to read more about Polster's ideas on bringing the client's story to life, you can find them in *Every Person's Life is Worth a Novel* (1987).

What is fascinating to remember, however, is that the reverse is sometimes true. Sometimes a client can get lost in a mire of rambling detail which drains them and their counsellor of energy. This is the 'Can't see the wood for the trees' syndrome. In that case it is useful if the counsellor can facilitate an abstraction. For instance, Brian, also talking about an abusive father, had just such a tendency to deflect from feeling and action by over-detailing. The counsellor asked him, "Tell your father what he has done to you — in one sentence." Brian paused for a moment and then let out a despairing cry: "YOU HURT ME."

Intensifying an Experience or Enhancing Vitality

It is important to remember that, every time you suggest something to your client, it is, in a sense, a confrontation — an interruption to their process and an invitation to become aware, or more aware, of their experience. This is true whenever you choose to focus on a word or phrase, whenever you notice a movement or comment on a theme. As soon as you suggest that they do something differently it is an invitation to an experiment.

Thus 'heighteners' can be quite small suggestions to experiment. These would include inviting a client to:

▶ say it again and be aware of what you're saying;
▶ say that (or that word or that phrase) louder;
▶ slow down and say that again;
▶ breathe and say that;
▶ say that imagining him (her, them, mother) standing in front of you;
▶ stand up and say that;
▶ look at me and say that.

Do not forget that these are powerful interventions and may have as much impact as if you had made a real confrontation. They should be delivered with sensitivity.

Focusing on an Aspect of the Present — the Here and Now

Experiments are, of course, used to focus on some aspect of the client's present behaviour in order to enhance their contact with the world.

While Malcolm talks about how he is feeling he keeps staring at the floor and makes no eye contact with his counsellor. Experiments to increase his contact may include asking him first to look at the counsellor without talking; suggesting that he turns his back on the counsellor while continuing his conversation; requesting that he continues while increasing his eye contact with the counsellor; inquiring of Malcolm what it is he is seeing on the floor; playing with trying to get in front of his gaze and so on.

Focusing on an Aspect of the Relationship between Client and Counsellor

At different times the counsellor represents, for the client, people from the client's past and present life. Furthermore, the ways in which the client relates to the counsellor will be indicative of the way he relates to members of his family and the society in which he lives. It may be appropriate at times to focus on aspects of the way the client and the counsellor relate, in order to increase the contact between them or to become aware of ways in which past or present patterns and relationships are being repeated in the consulting room.

Paul is listing ways in which he feels let down by his friends and family. So often, it seems, he feels disappointed, but he does not say so. The counsellor asks him to think of ways in which he feels let down by the counsellor herself and to share them with her. At first Paul says "Oh, I couldn't do that" and looks horrified. The counsellor invites him to experiment. Paul says, quietly at first and then more strongly, "You have let me down. It's important that you remember what I tell you, and sometimes you forget."

Bringing the Past or the Future into the Present — the Then and Now

Latner (1992) says that the Gestaltist is interested in 'the experience and awareness of remembering', rather than what is remembered. If some of our energy is preoccupied with experiences from our history or anticipated future, it is not available as a resource for our experience of the present. This not only means that we have historical problems but, with diminished energy or awareness available now, we may well be creating another area which will require retrospective energy later. Contradictory as it may seem, these experiments are to bring fuller energy into past or future concerns in order to bring about completion and integration so that they will no longer impinge on the present. Difficult past events can therefore move from being perpetually relived to becoming memories.

As a child, Betty was often locked in the cupboard as a form of punishment and had consequently developed a form of incapacitating claustrophobia whereby she greatly feared being trapped somewhere and not being able to get help. One of the experiments used with Betty was to recreate in the counselling session one particular time when she was eight. In the original experience, Betty was so terrified that she was unable to make any noise at all. Now, in the recreated situation, she is encouraged to shout for help as loudly as she can. She chooses a member of her counselling group to hear and to 'save' her from the dark cupboard.

Fred told his counsellor that he had had several sleepless nights, feeling anxious about a forthcoming speech he was to deliver. He experimented with exploring both his most catastrophic and his most successful expectations in the counselling setting. First, he stood awkwardly in front of the group and allowed himself to spout gobbledygook, to insult his audience and to pretend to drop his papers and spill his water. He and the group roared with laughter. Then he started again. He breathed slowly and deeply as he took his stance facing the group. He made eye contact with them and began to talk clearly and enthusiastically about his topic. The group applauded.

Restoring Healthy Self-regulation

Focusing on Self-responsibility

One of the major ways in which we perpetuate unhealthy patterns of living is by denying our power to change our lives. We wait for someone or something to do the changing for us. The language we choose to use confirms and supports either our freedom or our self-restriction. Words such as 'one' instead of 'I', 'never', 'can't', 'have to', 'should', 'must' and so on maintain our passive position.

Ruth is describing the parting from her son as he left for boarding school for the first time. When she says, "At such times one feels so sad" the counsellor suggests that she say "I" instead of "one", and notice if she feels differently. Ruth does so and at first feels uncomfortable at the shift in focus. Then she begins to 'own' her own thoughts, feelings and actions and to take responsibility for them, including her decision to choose boarding school for her son.

Resolving Interruptions in the Cycle of Experience

Fundamentally, all experiments aim ultimately to improve contact and healthy functioning in some way or another. Sometimes it is appropriate to focus specifically on the interruption that accompanies the client's difficulty. Different types of experiment are relevant when dealing with the seven different interruptions. We offer some examples here. However, they come with a caveat. Do not rush to offer experiments to eliminate interruptions before you and your client have explored them. Of course, in some ways you will be testing and challenging interruptions right from your first session: you invite your client to feel and to be aware; you reflect her thinking back to her; you describe her behaviour; you invite her into contact; you ask her to assimilate, and learn from, her experiences; you expect her to support herself as a separate human being. In these ways, and others, you may be offering challenging 'experiments' to your client and you will notice if she finds these challenges difficult. If she does, it may be tempting to offer an experiment with the express aim of resolving the interruption at once. Interruptions were once 'chosen' because they were the best way of managing at the time. They will certainly be accompanied by introjects which provide the reason for the person's way of being. A careful exploration of the interruption, starting with, for instance, "I noticed your energy drop then . . . what happened?", will lead to an awareness of the underlying core beliefs. Awareness and understanding are not only more respectful of the person and how they are, but are also safer. It may be that the client would find that there are dire consequences for some core belief if full here-and-now awareness has not been achieved before a major change is made.

For example, Paul discovered that, when he was a little boy, he believed that he would be abandoned if he did not keep his mother happy by being constantly loving and helpful. As an adult when, as a result of counselling, he started to be assertive about his own needs, he became depressed and withdrawn from the world. Careful exploration revealed that he still carried the belief that he would be abandoned for being 'self-willed' and was, in a sense, bringing this about by his withdrawal.

Having invited caution, we now urge you to enjoy and invite your clients to enjoy the excitement of using what is happening *now* between you to invent and undertake experiments which will restore their healthy, vibrant functioning.

Jake dismisses a dreadful burn on the back of his hand with, "Oh, that's nothing much." The counsellor, to challenge his *desensitization*, invites Jake to 'become' his hand and allow it to express feelings.

Sarah, in the middle of recounting a nightmare to her counsellor, suddenly remarks on a new ornament on the bookcase. The counsellor, to confront her *deflection*, suggests as an experiment that Sarah, as the ornament, comment on her nightmare.

George is thinking of treating himself to his first new car but keeps remonstrating with himself for being so extravagant and selfish. The counsellor, knowing that, though George is very generous to others he seldom indulges himself, instigates an experiment involving a dialogue between George and the introject of his mean and miserly father. George imagines his father in the room and talks to him.

Connie tells the counsellor that she knows he is impatient with her slow progress. Knowing as he does that he does not feel at all impatient with her, and to help her to reclaim her *projection*, he invites her to sit in his chair and talk to the self-doubtful Connie, so that she begins to realize that the criticism comes from a part of herself.

Robert bites his bottom lip as he talks about his parents. The counsellor, to enhance his awareness of what he is 'biting back', suggests that he allow his lips to 'blow raspberries' at the imagined pair. In this way, Robert undoes a physical element of the *retroflection*.

Penny is constantly referring to how she sees herself and how others might see her. She is in a state of self-conscious self-monitoring. The counsellor surprises her into participating in a playful pillow-fight, during which her *egotism* is replaced by spontaneous delight.

Elizabeth often talks about her interests using the pronoun 'we' — referring to her husband and herself. She is encouraged to 'own' her independent personal preferences by enumerating some of the things that she likes which her husband does not, hence needing to use the word 'I' and diminishing the negative aspects of her *confluence* with him.

Through awareness, contact and experimentation, Gestalt counselling can transform:

▶ desensitization through resensitization;
▶ deflection through direction;
▶ introjection through regurgitation and selective assimilation;
▶ projection through reclamation;

▶ retroflection through proactivity;

▶ egotism through involvement;

▶ confluence through differentiation.

Evoking the 'Whole'

In Chapter 11 we talked about the integration of thinking, feeling and sensing. It is also important to focus on the integration of our behaviour as well as our thinking, feeling, physiological and spiritual experiences. Because of our temperaments and our childhood experiences, we tend to become 'top-heavy' in one of the areas to the detriment of one or some of the others. Gestalt experiments may be used to restore this balance where necessary.

THINKING AND UNDERSTANDING

At times people are so involved, even overwhelmed, by a situation that they feel unable to cope. In these circumstances the counsellor's role may be to provide the client with an opportunity to clarify his thinking. For one person this might mean expanding the range of his ideas and for another it may mean learning to systematize or strip away extraneous considerations.

James, while giving a confusing description of a cycle of behaviour in which he seems to be stuck, is invited by the counsellor to draw a diagram of the situation on the board. This visual synopsis goes a long way to helping both him and the counsellor reach new perspectives of the situation and a valuable insight into the way James is perpetuating the problem.

FEELINGS

The appropriate expression of feelings is an important aspect of healthy self-regulation. Babies spontaneously self-regulate through the expression of their feelings. However, the lack of suitable response from caretakers to these expressions in infancy and throughout childhood leads many people to shut down their feeling function. Ideally, a person's thinking and feeling capacities complement each other.

Ahmed complains that, although he feels full of tears, he is unable to cry about the recent death of his sister. Knowing that Ahmed and his sister had in common a love of classical music, the counsellor invites him to bring along a piece of music which Ahmed associates with his sister.

ACTION

Acting upon our thoughts, feelings and desires is clearly a vital aspect of holistic functioning. When these actions are inappropriately limited or distorted, experiments both within and outside the consulting room will be helpful.

Anne and her counsellor work out a programme of gradually increasing distances to travel in order to deal with her feelings of insecurity on trains. Because of her anxiety, this experiment is designed so as to include a 'security' item that Anne can carry with her and which she selects from the counsellor's consulting room.

PHYSICAL SELF-REGULATION

Physical expression is our means of communicating with others. Restriction and distortion of this capacity lessen our contact and impoverish our relationships with others.

Felicity has begun to reclaim her potency in the world and, although she has achieved a great deal both emotionally and cognitively, her body armour continues to reflect inappropriate inhibitions. She is helped to experiment with standing in various assertive positions and updating her body language to match her new-found potency.

Sometimes disturbances in physical self-regulation benefit from the services of a specialist such as a dietitian, an osteopath and so on.

SPIRITUALITY

With its roots in Eastern religions and philosophies, Gestalt can be a vehicle within which clients can choose to explore aspects of their spiritual growth. By and large, most clients need to focus on their groundedness before they can safely turn their attention to the relatively unknown dimension of the transpersonal.

Although Peggy has worked on her grief at the death of her infant son, her faith remains profoundly shaken. One of the experiments offered to Peggy was to take on the role of God and have Him talk to her about her baby. Through this, she realized that she had lost contact with her God and had started relating to a projection.

Promoting Self-actualization

Many of our childhood aspirations become hidden under the pressures and expectations of our environments. Clients may experiment within the counselling forum to uncover these dreams and personal potentialities.

David had followed his father into a financially successful architectural career but he was not happy. In the course of counselling, he experiments with images and fantasies of growing up again and remembers a period of his life at six years of age when he took enormous pleasure from making his own small garden. Discovering his lost love of gardening, he retrains and finally drops architecture and becomes a landscape gardener. In his new work he finds a contentment not before experienced professionally.

Promoting Choice and Options

There is a way in which all the experiments in this section may be creating new options. Every time our client is trying something in a different way she is demonstrating to herself that there are always other options. One of the major differences between the client and the counsellor may be that the latter is not limited by the client's closed option range. A potent counsellor can invent creative experiments which help expand the client's repertoire of ways of living effectively.

Andrew spends most of his time working or at work-related events. He says he cannot think of anything else he would rather do. The counsellor suggests he does an experiment in which he quickly and repetitively finishes the sentence, "If I had the time I'd . . .".

'Owning' Polarities

In the counselling situation the counsellor will facilitate the client's growth with experiments designed both to explore his avoidance of a particular polarity and to enable him to achieve a point of creative indifference in relation to the issues he is bringing to his sessions.

Naomi spends most of her life seeming very independent and being a resource whom many people turn to for help and support. However, she herself increasingly feels taken advantage of and uncared for. Her counsellor suggests she explore the other polarity by allowing herself to be picked up and rocked by her counselling group. This is one of the first steps in Naomi knowing both ends of the dependency continuum and gradually moving to a more central position, of creative indifference, where she can fully experience interdependence.

Warren says he does not enjoy being close to people. He would always prefer to be on his own. The counsellor suggests that he explore this polarity by exaggerating it. Warren begins, "I like being on my own, I'm perfectly happy away from other people. I don't ever want to be close to anyone. I will always be by myself. I won't love anybody and nobody will love me." Suddenly he stops and turns pale. "That's not true. I'm lonely." He begins to cry.

One of the most famous concepts in Gestalt is that of the polarized parts of us referred to as the 'topdog' and the 'underdog'. The topdog part of us, as implied by its name, is often those introjected voices in our heads that are critical, admonishing, punishing, moralistic, prescriptive and prejudicial. They can bombard us with rules and regulations, injunctions and prohibitions. The underdog, as the recipient of these messages, is that part of us which, while yearning for spontaneity and natural expression, unquestioningly complies or rebels in the face (teeth) of the topdog. Experimentally creating a dialogue between these two parts brings into awareness both the process of the inhibitions and the point of impasse. This often brings about the shift of energy necessary to break through the impasse.

While preparing for an exam, Brenda easily loses her concentration and complains to her counsellor that it is useless for her to sit the exam. The counsellor suggests that she uses the word

'I' instead of 'it' and from Brenda's reactions to hearing herself saying "I'm useless" develops a topdog—underdog dialogue. After a while, the counsellor invites her to say "you are . . ." while in the topdog position, rather than "I". She begins to hear and identify the topdog as the imagined voice of her highly critical father. This enables Brenda to move to a position of realistic self-assessment in which she realizes she is not useless and can quite competently sit the exam.

Exploring and Developing New Behaviour and Skills

Joseph Zinker (1977) describes the Gestalt approach as an integration of phenomenology and behaviourism. He says, 'a unique quality of Gestalt therapy is its emphasis on modifying a person's behaviour in the therapy situation itself. This systematic behaviour modification, when it grows out of the experience of the client, is called an experiment.'

Resolving Internal and External Conflicts

Many clients bring conflict issues to the counselling situation. The impasses in which they live can be between internal and/or external polarities, as mentioned earlier. Their thoughts, feelings and desires may be in conflict with each other or with the thoughts, feelings and desires of other people. Experiments within this range of problems are designed to bring about conflict resolution.

Steve says he does not have time to play the sports he loves. He spends much of his time trying to respond to the demands of his wife. When asked about his own needs, he says that he 'wouldn't think of' putting himself first; his wife had had a baby and was tired and needed him. The counsellor invites him into a dialogue with his wife, being first himself, talking to his wife whom he imagined sitting opposite him, then switching seats and becoming his wife. He told his wife that he 'wouldn't think' of his own needs and wants. The counsellor invited him to exaggerate a little: "I would *never* put myself first." As his wife, Steve realized how nervous she felt about his selflessness, and how much she expected to be 'punished' later by his martyrdom. Ruefully, he became aware of the potential truth of this and began to negotiate for himself more fairly in the future, rather than become the martyr.

Occasionally the resolution of an impasse is acceptance of uncertainty, however uncomfortable this may feel.

Michael is faced with the decision of leaving his wife or losing his lover. In the course of his exploration of this dilemma, the counsellor suggests that within the counselling room he enacts walking along a path that eventually forks, the one to life with his lover, the other to a continued life with his wife. She suggests that he spend some time down each path and report his imagined experiences there.

Creating Situations which will Strengthen Skills

Because of our life's circumstances, most of us have not had the opportunity to practise and develop certain desired skills. The consulting room provides a suitable arena for the recognition of these skills and then their practice and development.

Maureen is speechless in the face of heated debate or argument. She practises the art of answering back in various experimental scenarios, such as taking on the role of a leading politician in parliament, expressing her opinion to 'experts' whom she imagines sitting opposite her.

Completing Unfinished Business

As we have described earlier, there may be many situations in the past that require completion before we can totally devote our energy to the present. Using experiments with the guidance of a counsellor is one of the most likely means by which a person can achieve congruent completion and closure.

Sharon regrets not telling her mother both positive and negative things before she died. The counsellor invites her to imagine her mother on her death bed and to share fully with her all that was left unexpressed at the time.

Joan, in an earlier example, relived an experience of being molested by a gang of boys at her school. At the time she had been frightened and ashamed. She had run away, never to mention it to anyone. This incident had contributed to her growing up fearful about the world — especially men — and experiencing feelings of powerlessness. In her counselling session she expressed her rage to the boys and then role-played telling her teacher. It was the beginning of her finding a new powerfulness in her life.

Restoring Developmental Deficits

As children growing up, we are often required by the adults in our environment either to rush through or hold back from achieving our natural developmental milestones. This can result in areas of deficit which impede our adult life and the awareness required to navigate our adult developmental stages. Counsellors ideally have some training and understanding of childhood stages and the developmental needs of each stage. They will recognize and identify areas of deficit and design experiments accordingly.

Adrian spent much of his toddler time in a plaster cast to counteract his hip disorder and is aware in his adulthood of restraining his curiosity about aspects of others and the world. He is invited to ask members of his counselling group whatever questions he wants and also, as a robust two-year-old, to explore the contents of the cupboard.

Summary

In this chapter we have offered an overview of experiments. You, the counsellor, should gradually introduce experiments with your clients, checking with them to make sure that your suggestions are appropriate. Use your clients' feedback to guide you. You will find, as you become familiar with working like this, that some experiments flow quickly and easily and the clients' awareness and options are immediately and irrevocably expanded. Sometimes, however, a piece of behaviour or a habit of feeling and thinking is so deeply entrenched that an experiment, while apparently successful, seems to have no effect and the client goes back to 'square one'. It is important that neither client nor counsellor be discouraged at this. It does not mean that the counsellor was poor or that the client is not trying hard enough. Some of our most ingrained disturbances take slow and careful work. Exploration to increase awareness takes time and experiments will need to be repeated in many forms before the client is finally freed to be what he wants to be. Whatever emerges from an experiment should not be judged right or wrong, but simply *interesting*. It is what it is. The client is who he is. That is part of the fascination of counselling.

Part IV

EXPANSION AND INTEGRATION

Chapter 14

WITH THE GESTALT COUNSELLOR: A CASE EXAMPLE[*]

The Setting and the Client

The counsellor worked at a bereavement service which offered short-term counselling to bereaved people in the borough. It was funded by the local authority. The client, Alice, was a 58-year-old married woman, who worked part-time as an occupational therapist. In her spare time she worked as a volunteer driver for 'Meals on Wheels'. She had two children — a married son of 35 and a daughter, Fiona, who had died nearly a year earlier at the age of 32. Fiona had had epilepsy since childhood and had died of a fit while in the bath and alone in her flat.

Alice was the youngest of four children, two of whom were the offspring of her father and his first wife. Alice and her brother were the children of the second marriage. Her mother took her and her brother away from her father when Alice was about four years old. Initially, she had no memory of that experience. Her mother told her that her father had died. It was only years later that Alice discovered that he had not died then, but later. As she told the counsellor this, she said that she could have seen him again, if she had known that he was alive. Her mother had died 18 years previously, following a stroke.

Alice had no previous psychiatric or counselling history. She was seeking help from the bereavement counselling service as she had been experiencing despair, depression and an inability to be involved in her work. She thought that this was due to grief following her daughter's death and that she had not mourned sufficiently. She had had a medical check-up and was physically healthy, although very tired.

[*] We are indebted to Janice Scott for this case material.

The counsellor now takes up the account in her own words.

Assessment Interview

Alice was a well dressed woman, stocky and squarely built, with upright posture. She was comfortably off financially. Her face was lined a little and, at times, her eyes looked puffy and swollen.

She sat back in the chair with her legs crossed and appeared to relax during the assessment meeting. Her hand movements did not show specific repetitive gestures. However, she did have a mannerism of rubbing her eyes, in a specific, almost circular motion. She appeared to do this as if to reassure herself in some way. She had a clear voice but it was thin and sounded very much younger than her age would indicate.

Alice's breathing was shallow and when she was distressed she held her breath. In relation to self-support, she appeared to be almost totally self-sufficient, in that she behaved in such a way that she neither asked for nor received support from her environment. (I found it interesting that in this and future sessions Alice would bring and use her own tissues, rather than use the tissues freely available in my office. It seemed symbolic of the level of her 'self-sufficiency'.)

When asked what support was available to her, Alice talked of her husband Bob, who sounded somewhat withdrawn. Alice said that he 'takes good care of himself' following a heart attack three years earlier. She also mentioned her son who lived abroad and one good friend, who was experiencing difficulties herself, so that Alice did not wish to burden her by asking for support.

Alice was in contact with her distress and was finding life very difficult, as she did not feel able to control the expression of her grief. She was able to make contact with me and was articulate in describing her life as she felt and experienced it. I found her eye contact frequent and she was able to meet my gaze. Alice appeared to hear me well, rarely mishearing. She did not make a move to shake hands or in any way to have physical contact with me.

My Responses and Thoughts about the Relationship

●

My response to Alice was positive. I was interested in her and felt empathic towards her. I was aware of our age difference and wondered if she would be inhibited by the fact that I was much younger than her, although I did not experience it as a difficulty for me.

In relation to transferential issues, I was aware that her daughter and I were of similar age. I thought that this might become important in the course of the sessions, in that I imagined that I might represent Fiona, her daughter, in transferential terms. I also thought that the manner of ending the counselling could mirror the way in which she last had contact with her daughter. That is, Alice might leave without saying goodbye or end badly.

The Issues

●

Alice was presenting with an unfinished gestalt. She was in the process of grieving for the daughter of 32, who had died less than a year before. Alice could not come to terms with the fact that Fiona was dead. She hoped she would come back because "I've been good".

I thought that Alice probably had been restimulated in relation to events and memories of her childhood, such as the separation from her father and family life. Fixed gestalts of her childhood, which she had lost from her conscious awareness, suddenly began to move into Alice's awareness as she felt the grief of her daughter's death.

Agreement

I assessed that Alice was highly motivated, had some insight into her difficulties and was willing and able to enter a relationship with me. I thought that she would be able to make effective use of Gestalt counselling. Because of the specific focus of the work, I thought that short-term counselling would be appropriate.

We agreed to meet for 12 one-hour sessions. She identified her wants as follows:

1   To be able to function better at work. By this she meant that she wanted to be able to work with her patients, without feeling so anxious about the possibility of being upset by them.

2   To be able to feel and talk about her daughter.

Discussion of the Gestalt Assessment

When she felt stressed, Alice demonstrated a number of inter-ruptions to contact, which were signposts showing how, during her childhood, she had learnt to behave and be in the world.

Desensitization and Deflection

Alice remembered, when she was a child, looking at other chil-dren and seeing that they were smiling and realizing that she never smiled or felt happy. She noticed that children got a re-sponse from adults if they smiled, and began to practise smiling. In counselling, she had little memory of feeling happy. Alice said that she had no memory at all of the six months after she was taken away from her father.

Alice's language included a high level of deflection when she talked of herself, with the use, for example, of "one", "you" or "it". I made the decision early on not to continually ask her to use "I". I felt that such a repeated intervention would be per-ceived as a criticism, and might in itself be a deflection from her work. What I did was hear and respond to her, as if she had said "I". If she had been in long-term work with me, I might well have introduced interventions addressing her language of deflection. In the second session, Alice said, "As a small child you have had enough pain and you can't cope any more."

I believed that Alice had adjusted to her environment, in the best way she could, by preventing contact with her experience through desensitization and deflection.

Retroflection

The most destructive act of retroflection is suicide. Indeed, Yalom's (1980) definition of suicide is 'double homicide', while Perls (1947) states, 'Suicide is a substitute for homicide or murder.' Suicide was an option that Alice talked about in the third session. She imagined being on a mountain and yelling, "I hate this bloody world, I want out", and expressed a wish to commit suicide. I said that I realized that she was in a great deal of pain. I also noticed that she had sounded very angry when she talked about hating the world. I suggested that, if she thought about suicide, she might find it useful to think about who or what else she might be angry with. Although she talked about suicide in the beginning and during the middle sessions, she said in one of the later sessions that the frequency of her suicidal thoughts had diminished markedly.

Another way in which Alice retroflected habitually was in her inability to express her feelings freely and openly: "I've got very weepy eyes, tears are very close to the surface." And in the third session she said that she was beginning to feel angry about the way her mother had treated her, whereas, until this time, she had felt only guilt about her.

Introjection

Alice manifested many introjects when she was feeling sad and vulnerable: for example, "I'm wasting your time, wallowing, embarrassed. I shouldn't be doing this." She also had rigid introjects about caring for others and doing the 'right thing' (we began to refer to these as 'got to's'). She acknowledged in the third session that her mother told her that she 'should go out to work; take care of people; be a nurse; a teacher'. Alice herself had never wanted to be an occupational therapist. She had allowed her mother's injunctions to be so powerful that they had directed her choice of career.

The introjects that Alice voiced were indicative of the level of retroflecting she used. Introjects are used by the individual to control their organismic healthy behaviour: 'Underlying a retroflection is a toxic introject' (Smith, 1988, p52). By using the word "toxic", Smith conveys graphically how some of the covert or overt messages that children receive can be potentially poisonous to healthy development.

Projection and Proflection

In the first sessions, Alice would project her need for care onto others. She would begin by talking about a patient with whom she had been working who was experiencing a bereavement. She seemed able to give to others care which she herself found very difficult to receive.

Confluence

Alice described the relationship that she had had with her daughter. They talked together every day: Fiona lived five minutes' drive away from her. She would bring her washing to Alice's home, to use the washing machine. Here I felt Alice manifested confluent behaviour. Looking to the other polarity, Alice made decisions as a child which were relevant to the position of isolation.

She was a child in London during the war and, at the age of 11, thought about dying. She decided that the painful aspect of dying would be the leaving of things and people, such as her doll's pram and her mother. In the counselling she remembered that, as a child of 11, she made the decision, 'Don't love anyone or anything' and then dying would not be so painful. Perls sees this form of decision as 'the tragedy of the neurotic' (Perls, 1947): 'The tragedy of the neurotic is not that he has never developed love, nor that he has regressed into the state of a child — it lies in his inhibition to love and still more in his inability to express his love' (*ibid*, p160). It seems that Alice went against her early decision by allowing herself to love Fiona. Yet in the penultimate session she became aware of herself as 'being in a box on her own' — a consequence of her childhood decision.

The Counselling

●

First Session

"Can I just talk and cry?" Alice very clearly stated what she wanted for this session.

During this session she described the last phone call with her daughter, where her daughter kept apologizing to her with "I'm sorry, mum, I'm sorry" and Alice in the end said, "If you don't stop saying I'm sorry I'm never going to talk to you again." Her daughter apologized again, and Alice put the phone down. That was the last time that Alice spoke to her daughter. Alice began to repeat to me the questions she had been asking herself since her daughter's death: "I don't know how upset she was, I don't know whether she needed me . . . I don't know why she should have died, she'd had loads of fits . . . I feel guilty about everything that happened to my daughter, and I think it was my fault." Alice had put together the pieces of Fiona's childhood and her history of illness and decided that she was responsible for her daughter's epilepsy.

Alice also described how her 'got to's' were being shaken, and did not seem so important for her. It seemed that the immense shock of her daughter's death had unsettled the introjects she had lived by for so many years.

During this session Alice expressed a wish to remember aspects of her childhood. At the same time she was apprehensive and as we worked together she came up with a fine image. The image was of her opening a door, into herself and her past. We established that she had control over the door: when she opened it and with whom she opened it. This was the strengthening of self-regulation.

Alice appeared to use retroflection of blame and feelings of guilt to distance herself from her feelings. I suggested that, between this and the next session, when she felt guilty about the kind of life she gave her daughter, she remember that her daughter had said recently what a lovely mother Alice had been. I also asked Alice to think about what other feelings she might have, if she was not feeling guilty.

Second Session

"Is this wasting your time?" Alice asked me this within a couple of minutes. I asked her if I was doing anything that made her think that she was wasting my time. Alice said that in the first session I had asked her if she had someone else to talk to, and she had heard it as a suggestion that she find someone different from me. She used deflection in her language, such as "People don't want to listen to other people." When I asked if anyone in her past would have treated her like that she became sad and said, "That's the way you're bought up."

In relation to her support network she said that she had told one friend about how she felt. However, and in return for being listened to, she offered to help the friend. It seemed impossible for Alice to seek support from another person without giving something back. With me she wished that she did not cry, because she was finding it difficult to push her feelings away. During the previous week she had brought to her house the sewing machine that Fiona had owned. She took the cover off, and felt that she could have hugged it. It was as if she could smell Fiona.

She discussed death and attitudes about death. About her own death she said, "I think it would be very nice; the manner of it is quite scary but I think oblivion would be nice." We did discuss suicide and I asked her to make a contract that she would not harm herself or anyone else, intentionally or unintentionally, while she was in counselling with me; in other words, a contract to keep herself safe. She agreed. It may seem strange to ask someone to make sure that they will not do something unintentionally. However, I believed that, by including this notion, Alice was agreeing to remain alert to the possibilities of 'accidentally' hurting herself and was committing to making her safety a central figure.

Alice went on to say, "As a small child you have had enough pain and you can't cope any more." The time that she was speaking about was during the war: her mother worked in a hospital; there were no public gatherings; there was regular machine-gunning during the day and as a child she used to dream of dead bodies. In hindsight, I believe this decision to deflect pain was also related to her very shallow breathing pattern, a strategy she may have used to diminish the level of physical pain she experienced through the childhood abuse which Alice was to reveal later in the sessions. Alice described her numbness at Fiona's funeral, which I saw as another manifestation of her ability to desensitize.

Third Session

In the third session, Alice said that she had been able to really be with a grieving patient. For Alice this was progress, in that she felt less fearful of patients' feelings, and felt more able to cope at work.

She said that she had dreamt about Fiona the night after the second session. In the dream, she had seen her, and had given her a hug. The house where the dream was set was a very nice place. Fiona was in a long room with a wooden table. Alice had tried to put a beautiful necklace around her neck, but realized that Fiona 'wasn't really there' and the necklace would not stay. In the dream she knew that Fiona was dead, but had enjoyed the dream a great deal. As Alice described the dream she looked warm and happy.

I felt that such a dream was significant, because in it Alice knew Fiona was dead, while in the previous session she still expected Fiona to come back. It seemed that, gradually, Alice was beginning to accept the reality of her loss.

Alice went on to say that she was doing things without much enthusiasm. When she tried to do things that she did not want to do she felt sick: "I should be doing something much more reasonable ... like the housework, or something more useful." Here Alice appeared to be beginning to reject, emotionally and physically, the introjects of her life which made her feel validated if she was taking care of others: "I felt very dry and arid if I was not doing things for others." Spinelli (1989, p110) describes the self in this form of existence as 'both fragmented and passive, viewing others as the primary means of defining one's status'.

Alice again began to talk of her childhood. In between the counselling sessions she had had vague recollections of being told by someone who was really nice, "When you're a grown girl, come home." She connected to this and felt that it was a memory of her father. She was aware of a 'comforting feeling'. This was the first time in her current awareness that she had any memory of her father.

She then began to talk about her mother and her memories. I include this passage as I think it graphically describes some of her experiences: "You take it [Alice as a child] out of its home, you dunk it down among strangers, you leave it, it's exposed to all sorts of dreadful things, . . . and then a mother comes back and pats you on the head, and says 'I miss you' and 'I love you', . . . and I was always very grateful to my mother for rescuing me from something. . . . she was working hard to support us, and she told us what she had given up for us."

Alice said that she had felt angry with her mother during the week, and actually enjoyed feeling her anger. I felt that Alice was becoming more aware of her feelings. This growing awareness may have been the result of questioning her introjects. Alice also said that I was the only person that she did not feel responsible for.

Looking back on this episode, I feel that it was a true 'I–Thou' moment — that 'special moment of insight or illumination whenever the participants confirm each other in their unique being' (Jacobs, 1989, p29).

ALICE: I sort of think I don't have any responsibility for you.

ME: No, you don't.

ALICE: Because you said it was a bereavement service, I don't feel I owe you anything . . . I don't have to think, what does she need? . . . I don't have to worry about you ... I'm not responsible for you, I'm very pleased to see you . . . I just come here and talk for an hour about myself.

Her eyes lit up, her face broke into a broad smile and she truly seemed to revel in the idea that she was not responsible for me. I too felt the impact of her delight. It was a special moment for both of us.

Fourth Session

"I've been good and I think it's time she came back, it's long enough. I don't really believe she is dead ... I've been awfully good, I haven't cried this week, I've got on with my work ... please can I have my daughter back now?" Alice was distressed about the fact that she still thought Fiona would come back. We spent time exploring this normal process of grieving and as we talked Alice said that, even though the sessions were very painful for her, she could now think about Fiona without having to push her memories away.

She remembered 'aunties' who were paid by her mother to look after her and her brother. These aunties would hit her with a belt when she wet the bed (which she often did). Alice was between five and eight years old at the time. They were moved often to new aunties, because of her bed-wetting.

"In those days, children were there, if you got angry, you hit them. If dirty old men felt like feeling them up, they did." As Alice spoke she became distressed. She told me of the decision she made that she must have been a very bad child when so many bad things happened to her. She described her three different childhoods: a family and a safe home; the 'Dickensian time' where "people couldn't cope with me because I was a very bad child"; and then boarding school.

Looking back on the progress of Alice, I feel that the memories of her childhood were mood-dependent and being brought to awareness through the course of her bereavement. Daniel Stern (1985) discusses the phenomenon of mood-dependent memory, where memories can be invoked as a result of experiencing a particular feeling. He hypothesizes that the child develops what he calls 'representations of interactions that have been generalised (RIGs)': that is, an impression of a situation that has become part of the person's expectation of life. Such structures are not fixed and are susceptible to change. Stern suggests that, when an infant has a certain feeling, the feeling will call to mind the RIG which has that feeling as part of its content. 'And whenever a RIG is activated, it packs some of the wallop of the originally lived experience in the form of an active memory' (Stern, 1985).

Alice's grief over Fiona was restimulating memories and unfinished gestalts which possessed similar affects, such as the death of her parents and the experiences she had had at the hands of aunties, teachers and others.

Fifth Session

This session occurred on the day before the first anniversary of Fiona's death. As Alice approached this anniversary, she described what she was experiencing. The previous day she had been 'very, very sad', because she had seen someone who looked like her daughter: "It's like a physical pain, it affects the whole of you." I thought that Alice was showing an increasing awareness of her body sensations and also how her body voiced her psychological pain. She began to express a variety of introjects, such as that she was 'wallowing, self-indulgent' and so on. I said I did not know how much worse pain there is than to watch someone grow for 30 years and then see them die. I told her I did not think she was wallowing, and that I saw that she was in great pain.

I thought that Alice was thinking rather than feeling. I suggested that she experiment with breathing more fully, as she had a very shallow respiratory pattern. She described feelings of faintness. I opened the window and did not focus again on her breathing for that session. Although I did not realize this at the time, Alice had in a few breaths hyperventilated (see session eight for further discussion).

Alice said that she had decided to go to work on the anniversary of her daughter's death. I said that I was concerned about her working on that day, as she seemed so distressed. I felt that it was not useful or self-caring to be working with her patients on that anniversary. My impression was that Alice was attempting to deflect her feelings.

As she went on talking, she described her husband, who appeared to feel nothing, and her own grief which she said was 'the most tiring thing I've come across'. She moved from her present situation to her childhood. She talked (without describing any details of the incident) about something that happened when, as a child, she was in bed. During the week the memories had come to her while she was in bed. "Everything was coming up, betrayal and horror and fear and it was there for about 20 minutes or so. That's how I felt about one episode when I was a kid . . . it was the kind of feeling that there wasn't anyone that you could rely on."

Here, I imagined that Alice was disclosing, without using description, an episode of sexual abuse. I did not ask her what had happened: I remembered that she had specifically said in the first session that she had had experiences which she did not want to talk about. I felt that, if I was right, to ask her directly would have been an abuse in relation to her specific statements in that first session. I left it to Alice to make the decision about what she disclosed and did not disclose. In this way I hoped to give her a different experience of a relationship — one in which she had control over the level of intimacy of the content she discussed. Using the analogy of the door, Alice was able to decide when and how much she opened the door to her past.

She went on to say that people could take advantage of her when she was hurting. I asked her how I could do that, but she said that she did not know. As she talked, she disclosed her belief that she must have been an awful child and person to have so many bad things happen to her. I felt that, in attempting to complete a gestalt, she had made a decision that the experiences that she had had were because she was bad and at fault.

"The first bit of my life must have been very good, otherwise I wouldn't have survived it." I felt that Alice was showing a great clarity in this statement and it led me to conclude that her early life had given her 'enough' nurturing parenting to enable her to survive and create the life she had. Alice's loneliness in the present seemed intense. She said she had come to me because "I wanted to hold someone's hand, because I'm too damned childish to do it on my own." I asked Alice whose hand she would like to hold. She replied that she did not know, but then began to talk about her husband. She said that in the past she had come to terms with the fact that her husband would never be what she wanted, but now she was having difficulty with the relationship when he appeared to be so unfeeling.

During and after this session I found myself at times almost overwhelmed by the level of pain that Alice was manifesting. At this point I was unsure whether I was experiencing counter-transference or resonating with Alice's process. I did not wish to appear to be unable to cope with Alice's feelings, in the way that she had described with her patients at the clinic. Because I was unclear, I did not disclose my feelings. I was fortunate in that I went from this session to supervision, where I became aware that I had been restimulated to some extent in relation to my own experiences of early separation. In hindsight I do feel that some part of the feelings I experienced was the result of resonances and inclusion with Alice. I was thinking of Jacobs (1989) citing Buber exploring the concepts of inclusion: 'the counsellor must feel the other side, the patient's side of the relationship; as a bodily touch to know how the patient feels it' (Buber, cited in Jacobs, 1989, p45).

Looking back on this session, it was very hard for us both, and I think that was to be expected in some way, because of the proximity of the anniversary of Alice's daughter's death.

Sixth Session

"I went up to the grave on Sunday. I felt much clearer for going . . . I put on my coat and went. I bought her some pink geraniums in a pot." Alice talked about the previous session. She felt 'dreadful' and had taken the rest of the week off. A colleague had taken her some flowers and Alice 'cried all over her'. I felt that this was an enormous shift for Alice. She was no longer able to interrupt her need to express her feelings and was also open to the support of a colleague.

"I think that last week was some sort of . . . it was very bad last week you know . . . like when you burst, lance a boil or something." She talked about her reactions to the session and the fact that, after it, she had felt as she did when Fiona had died. But instead of telling herself that she had to carry on (as she did over the funeral) she let herself cry. Alice then went on to talk about her mother: "It was important to think that we were friends with her [because they did not see her very often] and we got a hug. When you have a little bit of time then you want that time to be really good. And if she was displeased, you'd just be left with just the displeasure. If she was pleased with me, then I could go on through the week." I said that children will take what they can and survive and she responded, "Poor little thing, though."

Stern (1985) describes the function of the 'evoked companion' of the child, where, when the child is alone, they have the capacity to bring into their reality the parent, to counteract the feelings of aloneness. With Alice this seems to operate in two ways. When she had a last memory of her mother which was nurturing, she could evoke the nurturing parent; when displeased, she could only evoke the displeased parent. Alice took what nurturing she could from a variety of sources. Beaumont (1991) and Yontef (1983) agreed with Winnicott (1958) that a child with 'good enough' parenting, will survive: 'given a certain amount of parenting the child is not beyond hope and does have choice' (Yontef, 1983, p69).

Seventh Session

That week, Alice had realized more fully that Fiona would not be coming back. She had also realized that she was trying to find someone to blame for her daughter's death. I think this was a significant step forward, because for the first time (in the sessions) she was trying to find somebody else to blame instead of blaming herself. She remembered thinking of Fiona's boyfriend and had found a reason to blame him, as he had not been with Fiona when she had had the attack. When she alighted on a possible reason related to the boyfriend, she felt 'released in her whole body', as though in finding someone else to blame she could let go of the self-blame. She went on to repeat that she had blamed herself since Fiona's death.

This undoing of her retroflection reflects Perls' idea that 'an over-stern conscience can be cured only when self-reproach changes into object approach' (Perls, 1947, p159), where 'object' refers to another person.

Besides Alice's anger with Fiona's boyfriend, Alice also disclosed for the first time that soon after her death she had felt angry with Fiona. Again, I saw Alice making significant changes in the way she was contacting her feelings and thoughts. My concern was to ensure that the undoing of the retroflections took place very slowly. Perls *et al* (1951) are very clear in stating that the undoing of a retroflective pattern must be carried out with care, otherwise the personality of the client 'comes to its defence as if to head off catastrophe' (Perls *et al*, 1951).

However, further on in the session, Alice began blaming herself again, this time for being the kind of mother her mother was. I was aware that she was angry and was also retroflecting anger and blame again. I also felt that she was being angry with herself in a way that had not been possible with her own mother. I told Alice what I thought was happening. Alice responded by beginning to feel physically sick and faint. I realized that this intervention was too soon, even though Alice had repeatedly brought up issues of her childhood and parenting. She coped by feeling sick, which resulted in our concern moving away from the issue and onto carrying out strategies which made her feel more comfortable, such as opening a window.

Alice's behaviour led me to think that she had very powerful introjects about not expressing anger to her mother or others. If such introjects are not adhered to a high level of anxiety can occur. Smith (1988) wrote that, when an introject is not obeyed, 'The threat is experienced as if something awful, terrible, even catastrophic will happen.' In the light of such an observation, Alice's reaction seems very understandable. She had touched a 'limit situation' (Levin, 1991), a point which she could not go beyond, and had regulated herself in the best way she knew how, by feeling sick. Alice began to use the analogy of digging too deep and her wish to keep the door closed. So I reminded her that she had every right to close the door whenever she wished. She also had the right to open the door as and when she wanted, knowing she could close it at any time.

In this session, if I had had a 'rewind' button, I would have used it. I was too fast and made an intervention which was inappropriate. However, Alice coped in the way she had learnt in her past and told me, with the analogy of the 'too deep digging', that I had gone too far.

Eighth Session

"I won't take my coat off, I'm not stopping" was how Alice opened her eighth session. She said that she was quoting from an old radio programme. She admitted that there was a part of her that did not want to 'stop'. She had again felt physically unwell after the previous session. She did not go to the doctor, as she said it was "a thing that I recognized when I am quite stressed". Alice said that her body tells her what is happening much more than her brain does. I felt that Alice's level of desensitization was markedly lower. I said I appreciated her ability to listen to her body and acknowledge her needs. I did establish with Alice that she had recently been checked over by her family doctor and no organic cause had been found for her feelings of sickness, which had increased since her daughter's death.

In the week Alice found that she could think about her mother "with a different sort of love, not a guilty sort of thing, and I really felt quite warm towards her". She disclosed that she did get very angry the previous week: "I even got a little bit angry with Fiona." As Alice said this she became sad and tearful. I acknowledged that she could experience her feelings of sadness and anger and still function. She described what happened when she allowed her feelings 'to take over': "My hands get very big and my head grows. Everything goes grey, distances change and I feel very scared . . . my head gets woozy."

She described how she had at times become a 'screaming, whimpering heap'. I told her that, as soon as she starts to feel that, she can bring herself back by using specific strategies. I emphasized her choice in this, and her level of control which she appeared to have over whether 'it' happens or not. Alice asked, "Is it a memory of being ill as a child, because that is when it first started?"

In supervision I had described Alice's pattern of feeling faint and having distorted perceptions. It appeared that Alice was hyperventilating. I was surprised and at the same time it made sense. Normally, Alice breathed very shallowly, only moving the top part of her chest. So asking her to take a deeper breath could result in her 'overdosing' on oxygen. If her body was adapted to minimal levels of oxygen and high carbon dioxide levels, any significant change in those levels would have a profound effect. What I learnt from this was that hyperventilation has a wide range of manifestations, from literally taking in a 'physiologically normal' breath to rapid excessive respirations.

Ninth Session

Alice expressed concern that she was forgetting her daughter. I had an impression that Alice was resting after what had been a very painful time. I said this to her. She took a deep intake of breath and visibly relaxed. Her face changed and she smiled, "That's what it feels like." Clark (1982) describes the cycle of grief and states that, as a method of organismic self-regulation, 'there are times to take an emotional rest, to retire into isolation for recuperation'.

Alice began to hint more and more about something that had happened to her and how she felt. She used the term 'sexual abuse' for the first time, and said that she was eight. I had not made any attempt to direct her in her disclosure. She went on to say, "If I know it wasn't my fault, I'd be very angry at people, not my mother, I'd want to kill . . ." When she said this I was very touched that she had the courage to look into her past, after so many years, and to see so clearly the function of her self-blame. I acknowledged that the capacity to kill another human being is in each one of us and that being aware of our potential for violence makes it far less likely to happen.

Alice talked of her shock at crying about her father's death, something she had never done. She described going to Somerset House to see his death certificate. She felt that the death certificate was the only tangible proof that he had existed. She said that the certificate had the number of children he had. I said that she was one of his children. She became tearful and said, "I want to be somebody's child." She quickly dismissed this, reminding herself that she was 58 years old.

Tenth Session

Two weeks later, as soon as Alice entered the room and sat down, she began the session. She began to describe a dream she had had two nights previously; she said she had dreamt about me. In the dream she saw a huge white bird, which she decided was a dove. She saw that the bird was me, and in the dream she was able to rest her head against the bird's breast and drop everything (her burden).

Alice was excited about the dream and its relevance to what she was doing with me. I was moved by the image but did not suggest exploring possible projections. Instead I chose to focus on her feeling associated with the dream, as her face was so animated at remembering the way she let her 'burden' down. She then noticed my voice (I was still croaking following a cold). I was very clear with her that I was being well taken care of, and that I felt fine to be with her. Alice immediately expressed relief that she did not have to take care of me and then went on to disclose her feelings of relief associated with her daughter's death. Alice felt that she did not have to worry about her as she had used to. She had worried, for example, about whether Fiona was well, whether she took her medication, whether she crossed the roads carefully and so on. I understood her feeling of relief and said so.

Alice then made yet another important statement about her experience of the sessions and of me. She said she wanted me to decide whether she should take two days off work to go away with a friend. She wanted me to make the decision because then she could blame me if her boss complained about her taking more time from work. Perls (1969) saw this form of behaviour as a way of relieving the individual's feeling of guilt, yet at the same time this behaviour diminishes contact functions of the Ego. He stated that this behaviour was the result of 'an insufficiently developed sense of responsibility'. His theory fits well here, for Alice then went on to say, jokingly, "I want mum to decide." For me this was a fascinating moment of insight. Throughout the session I had been aware of the possible transference issues which might occur. In the knowledge that I am about the age that Alice's daughter was, I had assumed that I might have represented Alice's daughter for Alice. I had never thought about the fact that Alice could see me as her mother. What is so fascinating is that, apparently, age and gender are irrelevant to the transference in the therapeutic relationship. For Alice I became what was developmentally needed, her mother. The fact that I was her daughter's age did not matter.

With Alice the unfinished situations of her neurosis which required finishing became the figure against the ground of her recent experience. I think that, in the striving towards health, clients will find what they need in order to be healed. And, as Alice said in the ninth session, "I want to be somebody's child."

Thinking about the times I listened to and tracked what Alice was saying, I feel that such 'empathic interventions' mimic the parenting behaviours for the baby. Both Stern (1985) and Mahler *et al* (1975) describe the reflective mannerisms and vocalizations of parents. I suggest that the counsellor, using such interventions, may evoke in the client times when they were responded to by another with such mirroring techniques. If the need for reparenting is figure for the client, there will be a swift development of transference, which the Gestalt counsellor must address, either overtly or covertly. Clarkson (1989) suggests the transference can be allowed as part of the resolution of the client issues. However, Alice had only two sessions left, so I made an intervention which I hoped would reduce the level of transference and possible dependence on me. I asked her to be her own mum and see what her answer would be. She very quickly said she would like the two days break, and would request them.

Alice described some warm and happy memories of Fiona and then said how she wished she really knew how Fiona was now. I asked her how her life would be different if she knew how Fiona was now. Alice said that she would feel great. I experienced Alice as searching for 'the answer' in the hope that, with the answer, she would feel good again. Spinelli talks about the activity that individuals take part in in order to avoid the 'not knowingness of life': 'To be authentic, we must concede that all our being-related knowledge is, and will remain, incomplete and uncertain; whatever meaning life may seem to have for us is our construction and that hence in an ultimate sense, our existence is meaningless" (Spinelli, 1989, p113).

With Spinelli's hypothesis in mind, I realized that Alice was depending for her future feelings on an answer she could never know. I told Alice that I experienced her as searching for an answer and making herself dependent on an answer that she would never ever really know. Again, Alice impressed me with the level of her insight. She responded, "Maybe I'm still avoiding the fact that Fiona is dead. As long as I keep searching I don't need to face it . . . It's very difficult to live in the now, maybe it's easier to be searching for something that doesn't exist, than look at life as it is." If Spinelli needed an example to illustrate his concept, Alice had just given it.

Alice began to talk about her husband, who had cried a few times recently. She seemed puzzled by his crying, as he had not cried during most of the year after Fiona's death. I suggested that he might be picking up changes in her and feel more able to cry with her. I said that people change as they are with each other. I said that I had changed by being with Alice, as she might change by being with me: 'being' with another is in itself a change process. Alice agreed and said that she had changed and was changing. She said that she had been more friendly towards her husband.

Eleventh Session

Alice had had a good Christmas and had also felt sad at times. She realized that she could have a good time and still feel sad. She described her sadness as moving into warmth. She also talked of the kindness of others, 'half saddening and half warming'. She was aware that, when she puts her sadness aside, it builds up. As a child she had learnt that to cry was 'artificial': "If you must cry, do it on your own, not in front of other people."

ALICE: But it's OK to cry here.
ME: I think healing may come with crying with someone else.

There is something very healing about crying, being heard and tears seen.

ALICE: Why is that?

ME: My first thought is because we are human.

ALICE: Yes, that's a marvellous thought. We are so far away from being really human, trying to behave like machines . . . I want to find a group of people that don't particularly want anybody to be anything, with no expectations . . . I'd just like to be with people where I could be.

In this session I affirmed Alice's courage and motivation in coming to the sessions with me. Alice stopped breathing for a few seconds. Such positive feedback was overwhelming for her, and I remembered earlier sessions when she had also deflected positive comments of mine. I was reminded through this interaction that compliments given to someone who is not accustomed to receiving them can be as threatening as criticisms, if not more so.

Alice seemed to be withdrawing, and beginning to look at the future. She was showing self-support, and talked about joining a women's group. The energy level of the session was calm and I felt she was moving well towards closure.

Twelfth Session

"So this is your last session," I said. Alice spent some of the time looking to the future, at how she wanted to prepare for retirement, perhaps with the future support of more counselling. I do not think that she was deflecting from the reality of the last session, rather using me as a resource to discuss other possible forms of counselling, for example in a group.

She reviewed her time with me, remembering how she cried about her daughter in the first session, which had truly surprised her. She talked about the pain she had experienced and the depths that she had gone to. She described her difficulty in trusting anyone to see her; that she would rather run away. I asked her what it was like to be with me. She said it was different with me.

In this session I reminded Alice of her contract in our second session — to keep safe while she was in counselling. Before I had finished she smiled and stated firmly that she had no intention of dying until she was of a good, old age.

As the session moved to a close I asked her if she wanted to say anything or wanted anything from me. She did not believe she did; she said she always tried to say things at the time, rather than have regrets later. Which is one reason why it was so difficult for her when Fiona died.

I said that I had learnt from her. She was surprised and asked what. Remembering her difficulty in hearing positives, I gently said that I had learnt about the level of motivation someone can have for working in the 12 sessions. And I said I had learnt about courage. She looked down and was silent. She then returned my gaze, her face warmed and her eyes sparkled.

ALICE: You've changed . . . you're my daughter's age, about 30.
ME: I'm 36.
ALICE: You don't look stressed enough to be 36 [*laughing*] . . . I've never seen you before . . . you look merry . . . you suit that colour . . . I've never really seen you, just a haze . . . weird.
ME: Feels delightful.
ALICE: It was you saying that you have learnt from me. It's like sharing personal . . . I'm not your client any more . . . you're another adult . . . if I meet you again, I won't be your client.

This was really a lovely moment, a moment of 'pure contact'. Minutes later, I said goodbye.

I was very excited. Alice had come to me saying that she wanted someone's hand to hold and I assumed she was talking unconsciously about her mother. In the light of what happened I suggested that she had created what she had been searching for, a mother to hold her hand. And when it was time to say goodbye, she dropped the hand, saw me as me, and moved on.

Discussion

●

Throughout this work the counsellor was guided by a statement of Gary Yontef (cited in Mulgrew & Mulgrew, 1987) who said that a goal of Gestalt practice is 'to enable distressed individuals to experience fuller contact with their worlds so that they can assemble or reject experiences appropriately'. Alice 'wanting someone to hold her hand' had been a very clear request. She approached the counsellor five weeks before the first anniversary of her daughter's death. The issues of her childhood, the way she had learned to be, to express feelings, to behave in the world at large — all impinged on her present life experience.

The counsellor judged that the relationship between them would be the most important vehicle for healing, recalling Stern's (1985) concept of the 'evoked companion'. Alice had established fixed patterns of relating to people in her world which had prevented her from being fully in touch with her own feelings and needs, while also making her unable to accept support from her friends. Some of those fixed gestalts were changed in the counselling relationship in the movement towards a more healthy structure of self.

Making acceptance of her client's position the highest priority, the counsellor chose not to use many experiments. It is frequently useful in bereavement counselling to invite clients to undertake two-chair dialogues with the dead person. However, the counsellor thought it was more appropriate to allow Alice to talk about her daughter and her memories of what she was like rather than invite her to do two-chair work. To ask her to imagine Fiona in the room whenever she talked about her would surely have increased her strong introjects against expressing feelings. It might also have supported her disbelief in Fiona's death and her hope that, if she behaved well, her daughter would 'come back'.

Alice was in contact with her distress and identified her wants very clearly. She manifested a high degree of self-regulation in the sessions, being able to express some of her pain, then move into closure and withdrawal.

Perhaps the most important ingredient of the counselling was Alice's motivation. A client with low motivation will disempower the most skilled counsellor. Jacobs (1989) states that the counsellor is 'powerless to change the patient'. Alice approached her counselling session with commitment and courage. She may wish to have further counselling at some time in the future. However, the process of the counselling seemed complete; it progressed fluidly through the gestalt cycle of awareness. Alice came knowing what she wanted, addressed it and, to all intents and purposes, got what she wanted and finally withdrew.

Chapter 15

SUGGESTIONS FOR A COUNSELLOR'S DEVELOPMENT

Training
●

Encouraged by some of Perls' unorthodox demonstrations, some Gestaltists believed that theory, planning and formal training were irrelevant and contrary to the concept of spontaneity. A natural intuition and a willingness to go with the moment seemed all that was necessary. As we have said, Perls himself is often quoted as saying, 'Lose your mind and come to your senses'. However, people sometimes overlook the fact that Perls could use his intuition creatively because it was stabilized by a solid foundation of clinical training and experience. He was not just coming from a position of good intention and spontaneity. This was the 'figure' set in the 'ground' of his extensive knowledge and skills developed over years of analysis, training and integration of ideas and practice.

We believe that a basic training is essential to ensure competence. The acquisition of a sound theoretical understanding of Gestalt, practical counselling skills and the opportunity to put those skills into practice in a safe and supportive environment are all provided by such training. There are excellent trainings in Gestalt psychotherapy and counselling throughout the United Kingdom, Europe, the United States and Canada. We have listed the address of the Gestalt Psychotherapy Training Institute at the end of this chapter. The GPTI will provide a list of recognized Gestalt trainers in the UK. We also list some of the training centres with which we have personal contact. All of these centres offer core Gestalt training. However, there are many different emphases of focus, orientation and perspective and, indeed, lively arguments from time to time. We suggest that, at some time during your training, you sample a variety of approaches in order to get an overview of the field.

For further reading in English of the most up-to-date developments in Gestalt theory and practice, we recommend the *British Gestalt Journal* and the American *The Gestalt Journal*, whose addresses are also listed at the end of this chapter.

Supervision

Supervision is a basic requirement of Gestalt training institutes once the student is ready to begin working with clients and, we believe, should continue throughout a counsellor's career. It provides both the student counsellor and the qualified counsellor with a continuing overview of their competency in their work, an opportunity for the continuing development of understanding and skills, a forum to find support, challenge and encouragement and a necessary monitoring of the work the counsellor is doing with their clients. It is also a place to look at any practical or ethical issues that may arise in the counselling and to ensure that good boundaries are being applied. All counsellors should belong to at least one of the professional counselling or psychotherapy bodies, which provide a clear code of ethics.

Personal Counselling or Psychotherapy

Having your own personal counselling or psychotherapy is a requirement of training. Having first-hand experience of being on the 'other side' of the counselling relationship helps to create a far greater empathic understanding of your clients' experience. What may seem no big deal from the professional's side may seem very different from the other. Your own experience provides an inner map of what counselling is like, one which will prove invaluable when working with clients. It also provides you with a model of a counsellor: what is it that they do or say that you find useful; how does their personal style affect the relationship; is this how you want to be in your role as a counsellor? It may be useful over a longer period of time to be in therapy with different counsellors. This will help you to experience a range of styles and approaches with which you can inform your own practice. If you are practising with individual clients, your personal experience of counselling should be with an individual counsellor. Likewise, if working with groups, this should be the format for your own counselling. We recommend strongly that you experience both as you progress through your training.

Another important aspect of doing your own personal work in counselling is to free yourself from your own limitations and fixed gestalts or 'blind spots', so that your energy can be used unreservedly on behalf of the client. The more you work through your own issues, the less likely you are to impose or project your own issues onto the client. Awareness of your own process and 'stuck points' brought to light in your personal counselling and supervision will help you to use your responses to your client (your counter-transference) to facilitate their growth and change — and not to transfer inadvertently your own issues onto them. During counselling or psychotherapy past developmental deficits and traumas can be healed so that present energy can be fully used to deal with the continuing developmental needs and challenges of your clients.

But apart from the value to you as a counsellor, your counselling should have enormous value to you as a person. After all, if you believe it is good for others, why should it not be good for you too? In this respect, we believe it is important for you to undergo your own counselling or psychotherapy, not just because it is a course requirement, but because you want to free yourself from your own limitations *for you*.

Addresses

●

United Kingdom

Gestalt Psychotherapy Training Institute in the United Kingdom,
2 Bedford Street,
London Road,
Bath BA1 6AF
Tel: 01225 482135

The Metanoia Institute,
13 North Common Road,
Ealing,
London W5 2QB
Tel: 0181-579 2505

Gestalt South West,
79 Effingham Road,
Bishopston,
Bristol BS6 5AY
Tel: 0117 942 6938

The Manchester Gestalt Centre,
7 Norman Road,
Rusholme,
Manchester M14 5LF
Tel: 0161-257 2202

Stockton Centre for Psychotherapy & Counselling,
77 Acklam Road,
Thornaby-on-Tees,
Cleveland TS17 7BD
Tel: 01642 649004

Sherwood Psychotherapy Training Institute,
Thiskney House,
2 St James Terrace,
Nottingham NG1 6FW
Tel: 0115 924 3994

The Gestalt Centre,
64 Warwick Road,
St Albans,
Herts AL1 4DL
Tel: 01727 864806

Cambridge GATE,
Sparrow's Lodge,
Green Lane,
Fowlmere, Nr Royston,
Herts SG8 7QP
Tel: 01763 208291

The British Association for Counselling,
1 Regent Place,
Rugby CV21 2PJ
Tel: 01788 578328

United States of America

The Center for Gestalt Development
PO Box 990
Highland
New York 12528

Gestalt Institute of Cleveland
1588 Hazel Drive
Cleveland
Ohio 44106

Gestalt Therapy Institute of Los Angeles
1460 7th Street
Suite 301
Santa Monica
California 90401

Gestalt Training Centre – San Diego
PO Box 2189
La Jolla
California 92038

**PO Box 20742
New York 10025**

Canada

The Vancouver Gestalt Training Institute
1747 Gordon Avenue
West Vancouver
British Columbia V7V 1V4

Europe

Gestalt Counselling Centre of Rome
Via Della Divisione Torino, 47 (Eur)
0013 Rome
Italy

IGOR (Institut fur Gestaltorientierte Organisationsberatung)
Wolfsgangstr 58
D-60322 Frankfurt
Germany

Institut Francais de Gestalt-Therapie
8 Rue Paul-Louis Lande
33000 Bordeaux
France

Insituto di Gestalt
Via OM Corbino
5-97100 Raguasa
Italy

Multi-di-mens
Hertstraat 50
9000 Gent
Belgium

OAGG – Fachsektion fur Integrative Gestalttherapie
Lenaugasse 3
A-1030 Vienna
Austria

Journals

●

British Gestalt Journal,
PO Box 2994,
London N5 1UG
Tel: 0117 924 0126

The Gestalt Journal (American),
PO Box 990,
Highland,
New York 12528 0990
Tel: 0101 914 691 7192

Appendix I: Assessment Checklist

Contact Functions
LOOKING When does the client look at/avoid looking at me? How does he look (furtively, directly, etc)? What emotions is he expressing with his look?
TALKING Description of voice. What emotions is she expressing? How does she use language? What words and characteristic phrases does she use? Is her use of words flat, image-full, matter-of-fact, poetic, etc? Does she use language for gaining information, communication, entertainment or effect? Is her choice of words 'responsible' ('owning' her own experience) or deflecting? Is she clear, precise, understandable, or vague, generalizing, confusing?
LISTENING Does he seem to hear me easily? Do I have to repeat myself? Does he hear something other than what I say?
TOUCHING How does she respond to my touch (eg. handshake)? Does she seem to invite or shun touch? Do I want to touch/be touched by her? How does she touch (firmly, tentatively, warmly, etc)?

APPEARANCE

What can I learn from his dress, hair, skin tone, features, movement qualities, stance and posture, body splits (left/right, top/bottom, back/front)?

Is his visual presentation consistent with what he says about himself?

Support Functions

How does she use environmental support, such as the chair or cushions that she is sitting on?

How does she support herself? Rigidly, sitting straight up, or does she loll about, relying on the environment for her support?

How does she support herself with her breathing? Is it deep or shallow, does she take in confidently from the environment or does she snatch her breath? Is her speech supported by her breathing?

Do I feel I have to support her (being tactful, gentle, reassuring, etc)?

Does she seem to need to support me?

How do the above change during moments of anxiety (silence, questions, memories)?

Daily support: what support network does she maintain (friends, relationships, etc)?

How does she support herself in excitement or difficulty (friends, alcohol, drugs, exercise, television, eating, sleeping, etc)?

The Field

What life events/circumstances are affecting him?

Are there any political or social circumstances which may have a particular influence on his state of mind at the moment?

What cultural influences and pressures are relevant?

My Response

How do I feel in response to any of the above?

Who or what does she remind me of?

What counter-transference issues are likely to arise?

Awareness Cycle

Does he have clear sensations?
Does he know what his sensations mean?
Does he know what he feels?
Can he report on or express his feelings and thoughts?
Does he understand his own needs?
Does he seem to be able to mobilize himself?
Does he assess and plan effectively?
Does he take appropriate actions?
Does he seem to make effective contact?
Does he experience satisfaction afterwards?
Does he allow himself to withdraw appropriately and with ease?
In what areas of his life does he move/not move easily through the cycle?
Does he become agitated if questioned about his inner world?
Can I follow his meaning making?
Are the feelings he has congruent with what he is talking about?

Interruptions

Which interruptions am I most aware of in her interactions?
In what circumstances does she demonstrate these most?
How can I restate her presenting problems in terms of interruptions?

Presenting (or Emerging) Reasons for Wanting Counselling

Can I understand his reasons for coming to see me, and restate them with him?
What is the 'content': that is, what issues, symptoms, unfinished business, problems, experienced difficulties are to be addressed?
How do I link that to the 'process', as described above: self- functioning, interruptions, contact functions, relationship to the world, self-support?

Overview

Given all of the above, what areas of her life seem to demand attention; what seems missing that would enhance her life; which ways in which she impairs her contact will provide a focus for the work? What goals have I agreed with the client?

Reproduced, with permission, from Greenway I, *Assessment Checklist*, Sherwood Institute, Nottingham, 1992.

Appendix II: Client Intake Sheets

Sheet 1

Name	
Address	
Tel: (Home) **(Work)**	
DOB	**Age**
Family doctor **Address/Tel**	
Date first seen	
Referred by	

(This sheet must be stored separately from case notes)

© P Joyce, 1992. You may photocopy this Client Intake Sheet for instructional use only.

Sheet 2

First name or code	
Date started counselling	
Occupation	
Relationship status	Children
Parents	
Siblings	
Medical/Psychiatric history	
Drink/Drugs/Suicide attempts/Self-harm history	
Current level of functioning and stress	
Previous therapy/counselling	
Presenting issues/problems	
Expectations and desired outcome of therapy	
Contract Frequency and duration	Fee
(1) No violence to self, counsellor or room. (2) Limits of my confidentiality: (a) supervision (b) danger. (3) Four-week notice of stopping. (4) Cancellation and mixed appointments policy. (5) Taping and written material can be used for professional presentation.	

© P Joyce, 1992. You may photocopy this Client Intake Sheet for instructional use only.

Sheet 3

Contact functions 　　Talking 　　Hearing 　　Seeing 　　Touching 　　Movement
Self-support
Environmental support
Interruptions to contact 　Introjects, retroflection, deflection, desensitization, projection, confluence, egotism
Unfinished business
Impressions and reactions to client
Diagnosis and treatment plan
Points to remember

Reproduced, with permission, from Joyce P, 'Client Intake', *Gestalt Psychotherapy Student Handbook*, Metanoia, London, 1992.

© P Joyce, 1992. You may photocopy this Client Intake Sheet for instructional use only.

REFERENCES

Beaumont H, 'Fragile Self Process', *Workshop Presentation*, Metanoia, London, 1991.

Beaumont H, 'Martin Buber's I-Thou and Fragile Self-organisation: Gestalt Couples Therapy', *British Gestalt Journal* 2 (2), 1993.

Bettelheim B, *The Informed Heart*, Peregrine, London, 1986; first published by The Free Press, Glencoe, Illinois, 1960.

Bion WR, *Experiences in Groups*, Basic Books, New York, 1959.

Buber M, *The Knowledge of Man*, Harper & Row, New York, 1965.

Buber M, *I and Thou*, 2nd edn, T. & T. Clark, Edinburgh, 1984; first published 1958.

Clark A, 'Grief and Gestalt Therapy', *The Gestalt Journal* 5 (1), 1982.

Clarkson P, *Gestalt Counselling in Action*, Sage, London, 1989.

Clarkson P & Mackewn J, 'Fritz Perls', Windy Dryden (ed), *Key Figures in Counselling and Psychotherapy*, Sage, London, 1993.

Erikson E, *Childhood and Society*, W.W. Norton, New York, 1950.

Faraday A, *Dreamwork*, Pan, London, 1973.

Fish S & Lapworth P, *Understand and Use Your Dreams*, Dormouse Press, Bath, 1994.

Frankl V, *Man's Search for Meaning*, Hodder & Stoughton, London, 1964.

Friedländer S, *Schopferische Indifferenz*, Georg Muller, Munich, 1918.

Gelso CJ and Carter JA, 'The Relationship in Counselling and Therapy: Components, Consequences and Theoretical Antecedents', *The Counselling Psychologist* 13 (2), 1985.

Greenway I, *Assessment Checklist*, Sherwood Institute, Nottingham, 1992.

Harris J, *Gestalt: an Idiosyncratic Introduction*, Gestalt Centre, Manchester, 1989.

Hycner RA, 'The I–Thou Relationship and Gestalt Therapy', *The Gestalt Journal* 13 (1), 1990.

Jacobs L, 'The Dialogue in Theory and Therapy', *The Gestalt Journal* 12 (1), 1989.

Joyce P, 'Client Intake', *Gestalt Psychotherapy Student Handbook*, Metanoia, London, 1992.

Keenan B, *An Evil Cradling*, Hutchison, London, 1992; republished Random House, New York, 1993.

Latner J, 'The Theory of Gestalt Therapy', E Nevis (ed), *Gestalt Therapy*, Gardner Press, New York, 1992.

Levin J, 'Perls, Hefferline and Goodman', *Workshop Presentation*, Metanoia, London, 1991.

Levin P, *Becoming the Way We Are*, Transpubs, San Francisco, 1974.

Lewin K, *A Dynamic Theory of Personality*, McGraw-Hill, New York, 1932.

Lewin K, *Field Theory in Social Science: Selected Theoretical Papers*, Tavistock, London, 1952; first published 1951.

Mackewn J, 'Modern Gestalt — An Integrative and Ethical Approach to Counselling and Psychotherapy', *Counselling*, May, 1994.

Mackewn J, *Developing Gestalt Counselling*, Sage, London, forthcoming.

Mahler MS, Pine F & Bergman A, *The Psychological Birth of the Human Infant*, Basic Books, New York, 1975.

Mencken HL, in David Schiller (ed), *The Little Zen Companion*, Workman Publishing Company, New York, 1994.

Mulgrew E & Mulgrew J, 'Awareness of Self and Other in Gestalt Therapy', *The Gestalt Journal* 10 (2), 1987.

Naranjo C, 'Present-Centeredness: Techniques, prescriptions and ideal', J Fagan & IL Sheperd (eds), *Gestalt Therapy Now*, pp47–69, Harper & Row, New York, 1970.

Nevis EC (ed), *Gestalt Therapy Perspectives and Applications*, Gestalt Institute of Cleveland Press/Gardner Press, New York, 1992.

Parlett M, 'Reflections on Field Theory', *British Gestalt Journal* 1, pp 69–81, 1991.

Perls FS, *Ego, Hunger and Aggression*, Vintage Books, New York, 1947; first published in South Africa, 1942.

Perls FS, *Gestalt Therapy Verbatim*, Real People Press, Moab, Utah, 1969.

Perls FS, *The Gestalt Approach & Eye Witness to Therapy*, Bantam, New York, 1976; first published 1973.

Perls FS, Hefferline R & Goodman P (1951) *Gestalt Therapy*, The Julian Press; reprinted by Souvenir Press, London, 1972.

Perls L, *Living at the Boundary*, Joe Wysong (ed), p138, *The Gestalt Journal*, New York, 1992.

Polster E, *Every Person's Life is Worth a Novel*, W.W. Norton, New York, 1987.

Polster E, 'Tight Therapeutic Sequences', *British Gestalt Journal* 1 (2), 1991; first published in Zeig JK & Gilligan S (eds), *Brief Therapy: Myths, Methods and Metaphors*, Brunner/Mazel, New York, 1990.

Polster E & Polster M, *Gestalt Therapy Integrated*, Random House, New York, 1973.

Resnick R, 'Presentation at the Gestalt Conference', Exeter, 1985.

Rogers C, *Client-Centred Therapy*, Constable and Co, London, 1951.

Schiller (ed), *The Little Zen Companion*, Workman Publishing Company, New York, 1994.

Smith E, 'Self Interruptions in the Rhythm of Contact and Withdrawal', *The Gestalt Journal* 11 (2), 1988.

Spinelli E, *The Interpreted World: an Introduction to Phenomenological Psychology*, Sage, London, 1989.

Steiner C, 'Emotional Literacy', *Transactional Analysis Journal* 14 (3), July 1984.

Stern D, *The Interpersonal World of the Infant*, Basic Books, New York, 1985.

Wheeler G, *Gestalt Reconsidered*, Gestalt Institute of Cleveland Press/Gardner Press, New York, 1991.

Wheeler G, 'Compulsion and Curiosity — A Gestalt Approach to Obsessive Compulsive Disorder', *British Gestalt Journal* 3 (1), 1994.

Winnicott D, *Collected Papers Through Paediatrics to Psychoanalysis*, Tavistock, London, 1958.

Yalom I, *Existential Psychotherapy*, Basic Books, New York, 1980.

Yontef G, 'The Self in Gestalt Therapy', *The Gestalt Journal* 6 (1), 1983.

Yontef G, 'Techniques in Gestalt Therapy', *British Gestalt Journal* 1 (2), 1991.

Yontef GM & Simkin JF, (1989) 'Gestalt Therapy', Corsini R & Wedding D (eds), *Current Psychotherapies*, 4th edn, F.E. Peacock, Illinois, 1989.

Zinker J, 'On Loving Encounters: A Phenomenological View', Stephenson F (ed), *Gestalt Therapy Primer*, Charles Thomas, Chicago, 1975.

Zinker, J, *Creative Process in Gestalt Therapy*, Brunner/Mazel, New York, 1977.

Zinker J, Chapter 3, Harman RL (ed), *Gestalt Therapy Discussions with the Masters*, Charles C. Thomas, Springfield, Illinois, 1990.

INDEX OF PRINCIPAL
GESTALT TERMS

Helping People Change:
The Essential Counselling Series

These books on different approaches to counselling are of immediate practical benefit to everyone in the 'people business'. Written by experienced counsellors respected in their own field, each reveals a different way in which the user can develop counselling skills with clients. The series is edited by Dr Roy Bailey, a chartered clinical psychologist, counsellor, psychotherapy, trainer and hypnotherapist.

Practical Counselling Skills
Roy Bailey
The first volume to be published in the series, this book is an accessible and straight-forward basic guide to counselling, useful to beginner and practitioner alike. Group leaders and tutors running courses which include any element of counselling will also derive great benefit from this title.

Gestalt Counselling
Charlotte Sills, Sue Fish & Phil Lapworth
Covering both theory and practice this intelligible handbook offers a comprehensive guide to the philosophy and technique of Gestalt counselling for both novice and more experienced counsellors.

Transactional Analysis Counselling
Phil Lapworth, Charlotte Sills & Sue Fish
Transactional analysis counselling can be beneficial in a variety of situations, especially those of an organisational, educational and personal nature. This immensely practical guide contains the information required to implement this approach and is also an essential work of reference for the practitioner already using TA.

NLP Counselling
Roy Bailey
Counselling with Neurolinguistic Programming (NLP) refers to the assumption that all behaviour is the result of neurological processes that the individual organises into personal models and strategies. It is these strategies which the NLP counsellor and client address together: this book shows how this counselling method can be integrated into existing work with clients.

For further information or to obtain a free copy of the Speechmark catalogue, please contact:

Telford Road • Bicester • Oxon • OX26 4LQ • UK
Tel: (01869) 244644   *Fax:* (01869) 320040
www.speechmark.net